Postcolonial Struggles for a Democratic Southern Africa

T0314841

National liberation, one of the grand narratives of the twentie... weighty legacy of unfulfilled dreams. This book explores the ongoing struggle for legitimate, accountable political leaders in postcolonial Southern Africa, focusing on dilemmas arising when ex-liberation movements form governments. While the spread of multi-party democracy to most countries in the region is to be celebrated, democratic practice often has been superficial – a limited, elitist politics that relies on the symbols of the liberation struggle to legitimate *de facto* one-party rule and authoritarian practices. Using country cases from South Africa, Swaziland, Tanzania, Zambia and Zimbabwe, the collection explores three subthemes relevant to postcolonial governance in Southern Africa: how the struggle for liberation shapes the character of political transformation, the nature of rule in one-party dominant states headed by former liberation movements, and the processes of governance and resistance in post-liberation contexts.

This book was originally published as a special issue of the *Journal of Contemporary African Studies*.

Carolyn Bassett is Associate Professor, Department of Political Science, University of New Brunswick, Fredericton, Canada. She has published in *Canadian Journal of African Studies*, *Third World Quarterly* and *Review of African Political Economy*.

Marlea Clarke is Assistant Professor, Department of Political Science, University of Victoria, Canada, and a Research Associate with Labour and Enterprise Research Project (LEP), University of Cape Town, South Africa. She has published in *Law, Democracy and Development*, *Canadian Journal of African Studies* and *Work, Organisation, Labour and Globalisation*, and co-authored *Working Without Commitments*.

Postcolonial Struggles for a Democratic Southern Africa

Legacies of liberation

Edited by

Carolyn Bassett and Marlea Clarke

Routledge
Taylor & Francis Group

LONDON AND NEW YORK

First published 2016
by Routledge

2 Park Square, Milton Park, Abingdon, Oxon OX14 4RN
711 Third Avenue, New York, NY 10017, USA

Routledge is an imprint of the Taylor & Francis Group, an informa business

First issued in paperback 2017

British Library Cataloguing in Publication Data
A catalogue record for this book is available from the British Library

ISBN 13: 978-1-138-91344-8 (hbk)
ISBN 13: 978-1-138-08619-7 (pbk)

Typeset in Times
by RefineCatch Limited, Bungay, Suffolk

Publisher's Note
The publisher accepts responsibility for any inconsistencies that may have arisen during the conversion of this book from journal articles to book chapters, namely the possible inclusion of journal terminology.

Disclaimer
Every effort has been made to contact copyright holders for their permission to reprint material in this book. The publishers would be grateful to hear from any copyright holder who is not here acknowledged and will undertake to rectify any errors or omissions in future editions of this book.

Contents

Citation Information

The chapters in this book were originally published in the *Journal of Contemporary African Studies*, volume 32, issue 3 (July 2014). When citing this material, please use the original page numbering for each article, as follows:

Chapter 1
Introduction: Legacies of liberation: postcolonial struggles for a democratic southern Africa
Carolyn Bassett and Marlea Clarke
Journal of Contemporary African Studies, volume 32, issue 3 (July 2014) pp. 281–283

Chapter 2
Culture and resistance in Swaziland
Teresa Debly
Journal of Contemporary African Studies, volume 32, issue 3 (July 2014) pp. 284–301

Chapter 3
The Zimbabwean People's Army moment in Zimbabwean history, 1975–1977: Mugabe's rise and democracy's demise
David Moore
Journal of Contemporary African Studies, volume 32, issue 3 (July 2014) pp. 302–318

Chapter 4
Liberating development? Rule and liberation in post-independence Tanzania
Leander Schneider
Journal of Contemporary African Studies, volume 32, issue 3 (July 2014) pp. 319–330

Chapter 5
From liberation movement to party machine? The ANC in South Africa
Roger Southall
Journal of Contemporary African Studies, volume 32, issue 3 (July 2014) pp. 331–348

Chapter 6
A parallel universe – competing interpretations of Zimbabwe's crisis
Linda Freeman
Journal of Contemporary African Studies, volume 32, issue 3 (July 2014) pp. 349–366

Chapter 7

Land resistance in Zambia: a case study of the Luana Farmers' Cooperative
Grace-Edward Galabuzi
Journal of Contemporary African Studies, volume 32, issue 3 (July 2014) pp. 367–377

Chapter 8

Geologies of power: blood diamonds, security politics and Zimbabwe's troubled transition
Richard Saunders
Journal of Contemporary African Studies, volume 32, issue 3 (July 2014) pp. 378–394

Please direct any queries you may have about the citations to
clsuk.permissions@cengage.com

Notes on Contributors

Carolyn Bassett is Associate Professor in the Department of Political Science at the University of New Brunswick, Fredericton, Canada. She researches and teaches in the areas of political economy of development, globalisation and the political role of labour and organised social movements with a research focus on South Africa. Her current research is on the production of knowledge for policy engagement in the Congress of South African Trade Unions, and she is completing a study of popular budgeting in South Africa.

Marlea Clarke is Assistant Professor in the Department of Political Science at the University of Victoria, Canada, and is a Research Associate with the Labour and Enterprise Research Project (LEP) at the University of Cape Town, South Africa. Her work has focused on labour market restructuring in post-apartheid South Africa and the political role of labour and organised social movements in shaping the country's political and economic transformation.

Teresa Debly is a qualified high school teacher who taught English and Geography at Hluti Central High School, Swaziland, from 1987 to 1989. Since 2005, she has been actively involved with Swaziland Solidarity Network Canada. Her research interests include Swazi history, politics and culture, which culminated in her Master's thesis on the intersection of these three topics. She currently teaches music and continues to research protest music in Swaziland, prior to pursuing doctoral studies in Ethnomusicology at the University of the Witwatersrand, Johannesburg, South Africa.

Linda Freeman is Professor in the Department of Political Science and the Institute of African Studies at Carleton University, Ottawa, Canada. She specialises in African political economy, with a particular interest in southern Africa. Her study, *The Ambiguous Champion – Canada and South Africa in the Trudeau and Mulroney Years*, won the Harold Adams Innis Prize in 1998/1999 for best book in the social sciences written in English. Her current research interests include the politics of the land reform debate in Zimbabwe, the political economy of contemporary South Africa and more general issues of North-South relations. She is working on a manuscript on South African relations with Zimbabwe.

Grace-Edward Galabuzi is Associate Professor in the Department of Politics and Public Administration and a member of the Yeates School of Graduate Studies, at Ryerson University, Toronto, Canada. He is the author of *Canada's Economic Apartheid: The Social Exclusion of Racialized Groups in the New Century* (2006).

His research interests include the experiences of racialised groups in the Canadian labour market and the impact of global economic restructuring on local communities. He is also an active member of the social justice community in Toronto and has been involved in a variety of campaigns.

David Moore is Professor of Development Studies at the University of Johannesburg, South Africa, and has taught in Canada, Australia and at the University of KwaZulu-Natal, South Africa. He has published more than 25 articles and book chapters on Zimbabwe, and others on African political economy and development theory. He co-edited *Debating Development Discourse* with Gerald Schmitz (1995) and edited *The World Bank: Development, Poverty, Hegemony* (2007). In 2012 he co-edited a special edition of the *Journal of Contemporary African Studies* on 'progress' in Zimbabwe, with Norma Kriger and Brian Raftopoulos.

Richard Saunders is Associate Professor in the Department of Political Science at York University, Toronto, Canada, where he teaches African Political Economy and Development. His current research is focused on conflict minerals in the Southern African context, and the related emergence of regionalised political, economic and security networks around the mining sector. In 2013, he helped inaugurate a new two-year international collaborative research project on domestic resources mobilisation for development, under the auspices of UNRISD, Geneva.

Leander Schneider is Associate Professor of Political Science at Concordia University, Montreal, Canada. The main focus of his research is the politics of rural development in Tanzania. His articles have appeared in *African Studies*, the *African Studies Review* and *Africa Today*, among other journals. His book on authority, government and development in Nyerere's Tanzania was published in 2014.

Roger Southall is Professor Emeritus in the Department of Sociology at the University of the Witwatersrand, Johannesburg, South Africa, and, during 2013, was the Van Zyl Slabbert Visiting Professor in Politics and Sociology at the University of Cape Town, South Africa. He is a former editor of the *Journal of Contemporary African Studies*, and is author of the recently published *Liberation Movements in Power: Party and State in Southern Africa*.

Legacies of liberation: postcolonial struggles for a democratic southern Africa

Carolyn Bassett[a] and Marlea Clarke[b]

[a]Department of Political Science, University of New Brunswick, Fredericton, NB, Canada;
[b]Department of Political Science, University of Victoria, Victoria, BC, Canada

This special issue of the *Journal of Contemporary African Studies*, titled *Legacies of Liberation: Postcolonial Struggles for a Democratic Southern Africa*, seeks to explore the ongoing struggle for legitimate, accountable political leaders in post-colonial contexts where ex-liberation movements form the governments. The first two articles, by Teresa Debly and David Moore, investigate one of the main subthemes, the struggle for liberation and political transformation, in Swaziland and Zimbabwe, respectively. Three articles highlight the nature of rule in states headed by former liberation movements – all of which are now one-party dominant states – Leander Schneider on Tanzania, Roger Southall on South Africa and Linda Freeman on Zimbabwe. The issue concludes with two articles that use specific examples to highlight the processes of governance and resistance in post-liberation contexts, with Grace-Edward Galabuzi on the privatisation of Zambia's mines and Richard Saunders on blood diamonds in Zimbabwe.

The origins of this special issue are a series of discussions that began at the retirement of one of the Canada's foremost scholars of African studies, York University Professor John S. Saul; the theme of the special issue draws on key questions about the nature and legacy of liberation movements in Southern Africa that have preoccupied Saul for the past half-century. Saul has been one of the most knowledgeable, sympathetic and prolific chroniclers of the anti-colonial struggle as it unfolded between the 1960s and 1990s in southern Africa, highlighting problems that plagued many of the region's liberation movements once they gained political power. Key themes in Saul's works include the dialectics of leadership accountability and grassroots participation and the challenge of fostering bottom-up, genuinely participatory processes of social change. Though the authors in this volume do not necessarily accept Saul's conclusions or even his basic assumptions, and in fact not all directly address his writings, they do engage with one or more of these central questions.

Saul has been part of a generation of important western scholars of African liberation politics and perhaps the foremost critical researcher of radical liberation movements in southern Africa. A self-described 'revolutionary traveler' (Saul 2009), he not only documented 30 years of liberation struggle in the region, but also sought to actively support those struggles through his writings, his teachings and his ongoing engagement with the region from his base in Toronto, most notably with the Toronto Committee for the Liberation of Southern Africa (TCLSAC). Author of more than 14 authored and co-authored books, dozens of scholarly articles and even more popular articles and editorials on the region, Saul has been able to draw not only from decades of research but also years spent in the region, and a wealth of friends, contacts and comrades to present a strongly informed, sympathetic yet critical analysis of national liberation struggles and post-liberation politics in the region.

National liberation was one of the grand narratives of the twentieth century, yet it poses something of a paradox, because victory in a national liberation struggle is simultaneously an end and a beginning. Southern Africa suffered some of the longest standing colonial regimes on the continent and the struggles for independence from white settler rule proved to be long and bitter. Substantial white settlement in South Africa, Zimbabwe, Namibia, Angola and Mozambique (and to a lesser extent Zambia, Swaziland and Tanzania) rendered those colonial regimes particularly tenacious (Wilson 1994, 177–197). As recently as 1970, only Swaziland (nominally a 'protectorate' ruled by the Swazi king under British imperial authority which was heavily dependent on white-ruled South Africa), Zambia and Tanzania (both of which had seen only limited white settlement) were independent of European or minority white-settler rule (Hargreaves 1996, 200–247).

Many of Southern Africa's liberation struggles were led in whole or in part by exiled guerilla movements forced to operate in secret military cells that militated against consultation with the mass population, much less democratic participation and account-ability. The transition from guerilla movement to political party did not necessarily transform the political culture of liberation movements in any fundamental way. Even those former African colonies like Tanzania and Zambia that did not suffer the depredations of minority rule found the appeal of *de facto* or *de jure* one party rule, political centralization and authoritarian decision-making irresistible.

Victory represents an end in the sense that the old oppressive system has been overturned, denied and rejected. But it is a beginning in that what comes next has yet to be determined. By and large, southern Africa's victorious national liberation movements embraced a strong state and a top-down approach that prioritised leadership and nation building ahead of participation, democracy and voice (Melber 2003). When combined with the (usually) external imposition of economic restructuring programmes shaped by neoliberal norms, introduced in an equally top-down fashion and enforced by interna-tional funders and other foreign institutions, the challenge of genuine liberation for southern Africa seems all the more pressing today and yet more distant than ever.

John S. Saul often concluded his sometimes-discouraging analysis with the phrase *A Luta Continua* – the struggle continues. In many ways, his sentiment offers a way to situate this volume – many of the struggles discussed here are unfinished, in progress, and even, where successful, remain partial and inadequate compared to the monumental nature of the task. Moreover, the special issue is but one intervention in a broader series of discussions and debates on this topic (see, for example, Melber 2003; Southall 2013) and an incomplete one at that. Certain important actors, sectors and issues are entirely absent from this special issue, notably gender and the environment; others are addressed incompletely, and certain countries, notably Mozambique and Namibia, do not feature in the pages here. For this, we apologise and draw your attention to other fine books, articles and special journal issues that cover some of the issues and themes we have missed. Nonetheless, we hope you agree this special issue offers a substantial contribution to the debates on the legacies of liberation, the meaning of democracy in Africa and the significance of mobilisation. *A Luta Continua.*

Acknowledgements

The editors would like to thank the external reviewer for this entire special issue for being so generous with your time and for your very careful and thoughtful review of all these articles. Your comments, corrections and suggestions for individual articles along with overall suggestions on the special issue were extremely helpful. We are very grateful and thank you.

References

Hargreaves, John. 1996. *Decolonization in Africa*. 2nd ed. London: Longman.
Melber, Henning, ed. 2003. *Limits to Liberation in Southern Africa: The Unfinished Business of Democratic Consolidation*. Cape Town: HSRC Press.
Saul, John S. 2009. *Revolutionary Traveller Freeze Frames from a Life*. Winnipeg: Arbiter Ring.
Southall, Roger. 2013. *Liberation Movements in Power*. London: James Currey.
Wilson, Henry S. 1994. *African Decolonization*. London: Edward Arnold.

Culture and resistance in Swaziland

Teresa Debly

Department of History, University of New Brunswick, Saint John, NB, Canada

This article investigates the current political struggle in Swaziland, focusing on the role of culture in the growing resistance by youth and other opposition groups to the political repression and naked greed of Swaziland's monarchy under King Mswati III. As this article shows, to date, opposition groups have been thwarted in their campaign for broad, but fairly straightforward, political changes in Swaziland: multi-party elections, parliamentary democracy, increased rights and citizens' participation in politics. The article explains that the King continues to use (and manipulate) culture and tradition to justify his authority, in particular through institutions like the 'traditional Parliament', *tinkhundla*, and the state investment company, *tibiyo*. These are, however, not part of ancient Swazi tradition; they were created by the monarchy in recent history to help the regime maintain its authority. To challenge the legitimacy of the king's rule, the opposition also creatively uses culture and tradition. The article shows how political dissidents have used songs and music, especially at funerals of political dissidents, to 're-claim' culture and tradition in order to keep the struggle for political reform alive.

The Kingdom of Swaziland is often described as the 'Switzerland of Africa', which conjures up beautiful images of magnificent mountain scenery and lush green pastures (SIPA 2008, 6). Even place names, such as Ezulwini (the 'valley of heaven' – home to the royal family), depict an African Shangri-La. These euphemisms are strictly a 'view from above' and used by government, business and tourism offices to present the image of an idyllic place.

Daily life in Swaziland, however, is not idyllic for most people. The country has been, and remains, a very divided and unequal society run by the monarchy. In August 2008, Forbes magazine named Swaziland's King Mswati III the second richest man in Africa, while the United Nations World Food Program 'keeps a record 600,000 Swazis alive – more than 60% of the population' (Republic of South Africa 2008). Also in 2008, the United Nations Development Program reported that 69% of the population lived below the poverty line, while the king had between 14 and 20 wives and concubines, more than 20 children and more than a dozen new palaces (in addition to the one inherited from his father, King Sobhuza II). Further, the country has the dubious notoriety of having the world's highest prevalence of HIV/AIDS (Lewis 2005, 179). This socio-economic context has fomented a political crisis that has manifested itself in a struggle to define authentic Swazi culture.

At the centre of this political struggle is the country's monarch, King Mswati III, the last absolute monarch on the continent. When he ascended the throne in 1986, he did so amidst hopes he would rule differently than his father. Swazis imagined there would be positive change because the young king was 'modern' and had been educated in England. Yet his ruling style has not deviated from that of his father and his power, if anything, has grown over the past three decades. Like his father, King Mswati III has refused to introduce any reforms aimed at democratisation and instead has used a government-sponsored ideology of cultural traditionalism to justify banning all political parties and maintain a state of emergency. Despite decades of constitutional talks and the introduction of a new constitution in February 2006, political activists and lawyers believe nothing has changed because the king retains ultimate power over the legislative, judicial, executive, economic and security branches of government. His rule can be described as modern authoritarianism, cloaked in traditionalism.

Although Swaziland passed through a century of colonisation to achieve independence from Europe without bloodshed, the authoritarian nature of post-colonial rule has generated significant resistance, including an increasingly visible armed resistance movement. Perhaps more importantly, I argue here, popular uprisings and protests have grown in recent years, with youth and other opposition groups using culture as a way of expressing themselves and challenging the oppressive rule of the king. Indeed, it is this resistance – rather than more traditional tactics used by opposition groups – that seems to be undermining the confidence of the state in the king's ability to justify his political and economic activities as based on tradition and culture. This article explores these issues by examining the nature of political resistance in Swaziland, specifically its employ of cultural weapons like music, to challenge both the king's despotic rule and his own use of tradition and culture to smother resistance. If the state's overreaction to the singing of political songs at funerals is any indication, the Swazi monarchy is feeling extremely threatened by these so-called weapons of the weak and may find it more difficult to continue its authoritarian rule.

The article begins with an overview of the nature of the Swazi state, the regime and the nature of the monarchy. It focuses on two authoritative institutions of governance – *Tinkhundla* and *Tibiyo takaNgwane (Tibiyo)* – that are the locus of regime power and of resistance. These two institutions, which are protected by a discourse of traditionalism, enable the ruling Ngwane Dlamini clan to maintain their economic and political grip on Swazi society. As will be discussed below, *Tinkhundla* controls who can become involved in the political system while *Tibiyo* controls the 'wealth of the nation'. Although these institutions nakedly concentrate power and wealth in the hands of the royal family, their real purpose has been masked by the claim that tradition justifies the operation of these institutions. The article then turns to songs as expressions of resistance, and to funerals as their conduit to a public audience. These two sites challenge the state on its cultural terrain. Funerals have been one of the very last remaining 'free spaces' for public political expression in the kingdom and therefore have been important sites of resistance. Songs often are shared at funerals, and in Swaziland today, with its incredibly high levels of HIV/AIDS (estimated at 26% of adults aged 15–49 years), funerals have become weekly events. The efforts by the state to clamp down on political expression at funerals extends repression in Swaziland, but may also reflect the monarchy's growing lack of confidence that it can maintain its authority in light of growing and increasing public opposition.

Brief Swazi history

The Kingdom of Swaziland borders Mozambique and South Africa. It is 17,363 km^2, which is about one-quarter the land mass of Ireland, with a population of 1.2 million. Unlike most African states, Swaziland contains primarily one sociocultural linguistic grouping, the Swazi. The ruling Dlamini clan settled in south-eastern Africa during the late fifteenth or early sixteenth century, where the Swazi *Ngwenyama*,[1] or king, tried to consolidate land in the region. The Swazi state was never entirely secure due to Zulu and Ndwandwe incursions from the south. In 1854, after a devastating raid by the warring Zulus, *Ngwenyama* Mswati I appealed to the British in Natal for protection. The British were unwilling to take responsibility for protecting Mswati I's territory, but helped curtail the Zulu attacks. By 1861, Mswati I had begun granting land concessions to Boer and British settlers, strengthening the ties among Britain, South Africa and Swaziland. After the South African War (Anglo-Boer War) in 1902, Britain officially began to assume responsibility for Swaziland, which became a protectorate. The Swazi *Ngwenyama* became a 'Paramount Chief' under British rule, and over the next two decades, the Swazi people were 'separated into thirty-one different reserves with a total area of just over one-third of the country' (Potholm 1972, 15), losing much of their access to land to white settlers.

Shortly after ascending to the throne in 1921, Sobhuza II (1899–1983) began a lengthy but futile pursuit through the British courts to regain the territory of his forefathers. In December 1922, Sobhuza II and a group of advisors sailed to London to claim the British had taken Swazi lands illegally (Grotpeter 1975, 152). Early in 1923, they met with the secretary of state for the colonies and King George V but their pleas were rejected. In 1924, Sobhuza II undertook a 'landmark lawsuit' (Booth 2000, 270) that challenged the legitimacy of the concessions granted to British settlers during the reign of his grandfather, Mbandzeni, as well as the legality of settler colonialism in Swaziland. The case was decided in 1926 against Sobhuza II; he appealed to the Privy Council but was rejected in April 1926. In response to these losses, Sobhuza II 'changed his tactics and at the same time altered his persona, refashioning himself into an arch-traditionalist. Thenceforth 'traditionalism', authentic or manufactured, became both the essence and the basis of his political legitimacy' (93). Until this point, Sobhuza II had thought of himself as modern and progressive, but reverting to 'traditionalism' offered him a new strategy to press his claims against British colonial rule. Sobhuza II began to use culture as a 'shield' against the British, attempting to ward off both the land and resource deprivations of settler colonialism and the 'modern' ideas of parliamentary sovereignty, but, as we will see later, he also began to use culture as a spear against internal Swazi dissent soon after independence.

Sobhuza II's reversion to tradition failed to sway the British to modify the terms of colonial rule, much less withdraw from the territory, and it was not until the 'winds of change' swept across Africa in the 1960s that Swaziland was able to join its northern neighbours in embarking on negotiations for independence. The king soon found he could not wholly control the terms of independence from the British, notably failing to forestall the advent of political parties or an electorally based parliamentary system. Sobhuza II's fear of modern African nationalism and majority rule was shared with the white community, and prior to 1960, there had been no political parties in Swaziland. Sobhuza II claimed political parties were contrary to African customs and served only the interests of power-hungry individuals (Stevens 1963, 330–331). Yet, with independence and democracy on the horizon, several parties were formed in the early 1960s, including the Ngwane National Liberatory Congress (NNLC), founded by Dr Ambrose Zwane.

A referendum that demonstrated the support of the Swazi people for independence from Britain was followed by constitutional talks, leading to independence in September 1968. At independence, Swaziland became a constitutional monarchy with a Westminster-style bicameral legislature comprising a House of Assembly and a Senate. The new constitution negotiated with the British as the basis for full Swazi sovereign independence permitted King Sobhuza II to appoint 6 of the 30 members to parliament as well as 6 of the 12 members of Senate (Baloro 1994, 22). The political party that won the pre-independence 1967 election and therefore formed the government at independence was the *Imbokodvo* National Movement (INM), a party formed by Sobhuza II.[2] Most other parties soon merged with the king's INM, leaving the NNLC as the main opposition party. In the first post-independence election in 1972, the socialist-leaning NNLC won 3 of the 24 seats in parliament, all in the eastern sugar plantation constituencies where workers were dissatisfied with the government over working conditions.

Although losing three seats in 1972 did not pose an immediate political danger to the king's power, he refused to countenance opposition members in the legislature. Several attempts were made to limit the NNLC opposition, but each one was successfully challenged in the courts. Sobhuza II then opted for a new approach. On 12 April 1973, he declared that the constitution itself was causing growing unrest and permitting 'undesirable political practices'. Because, he said, there was 'no constitutional way' to amend the constitution, a new constitution needed to be 'created by ourselves for ourselves in complete liberty' (Kuper 1978, 335). Parliament passed a resolution saying the constitution was unworkable, following which Sobhuza II declared a state of emergency and assumed supreme power. Parliament was closed and remained so for five years (Vieceli 1982, 58–59; Ayee 1989, 56–57). Under the state of emergency, all political parties (including the monarchy's INM) and trade unions were banned, as were political meetings, processions and demonstrations unless they had the prior consent of the police commissioner. In addition, the king gained the power to detain a person without trial for a maximum of 60 days, which could be renewed 'as often as deemed necessary in the public interest' (Kuper 1978, 36). The state of emergency decree was to be reviewed in six months; however, it has never been repealed. As Baloro (1994, 26) put it, with the threat of indefinite imprisonment, the 'Government of Swaziland had enough weapons in its armoury to crush any form of political opposition'. Political opponents saw the state of emergency as one of Sobhuza II's many moves to strengthen the political grip of the monarchy: the event has been described as the 'king's coup' or the 'royal coup' (Vieceli 1982, 59; Jackson and Rosberg 1982, 129). The king's actions meant Swaziland effectively became a no-party state under the political leadership of the king.

Shortly before the closure of parliament and the implementation of the state of emergency, Sobhuza II had begun developing an army, the Umbutfo Swaziland Defence Force (USDF), to counter his 'lifelong mistrust of police loyalty' (Booth 2000, 13). This modern army, which made its first public appearance in the period immediately after the 1973 decree (Kuper 1978, 335), obtained its weapons and training with the help of Israel and apartheid South Africa (Levin 1997, 168). Although the justification for the army was unrest in neighbouring Mozambique and South Africa, the defence force would not have been sufficient to match either of its neighbours. Instead, it played an important role in helping to crush domestic dissent, such as the 1977 teacher–student protests and periodic labour unrest. Thus, the new army would help maintain the Dlamini family's position of power, as did *tinkhundla*, to which we now turn.

The genesis and transformation of *Tinkhundla*

Tinkhundla is best understood as a network of channels through which loyalty to the Swazi state and monarchy is recognised and rewarded with patronage, land and jobs. While *Tinkhundla* had only played a minor role in politics prior to colonisation and during the decolonisation phase, it began to play a central role in politics in 1973, when Sobhuza II abolished the constitution and transformed *tinkhundla* into an almost divinely mandated institution. When parliament reopened in 1978, *tinkhundla* was given a new, central role in the country's electoral system. As such, both the decree of 12 April 1973 and the institution of *tinkhundla* remain the central points of contention in contemporary Swaziland, and therefore the primary target to which resistance is directed.

The institution of *tinkhundla* had rather inauspicious beginnings. *Tinkhundla* is a siSwati word that refers to open spaces 'outside the cattle byre where men meet to discuss local affairs' (Booth 2000, 317). It has been translated as 'regional committees', 'regional councils' and 'royal administrative centres'. Its historical roots can be traced back to the mid-1950s, when Swazi authorities and colonial officials began turning former WWII recruitment centres into meeting places with broad 'development objectives' (Kuper 1978, 185). These sites were used to organise rural development projects and channel development assistance funding to rural areas. Local chiefs and other community members were encouraged to participate in such processes and related discussions. However, within five years, both Swazi authorities and colonial administrators effectively ended the system, which they considered to be dysfunctional. As Booth notes:

> *Tinkhundla* meetings were infrequently held and scantily attended. *iNkhundla* governors were considered lazy and inept. Furthermore, the entire system was viewed with such deep suspicion by chiefs as a means by which they were being bypassed by Sobhuza and thus rendered less relevant. Finally, in the words of one district official, 'the Swazi National Council [*libandla*] has jealously refused to delegate authority [to the *tinkhundla*] and its pathological reluctance to make decisions has brought … tribal administration to a state of affairs closely akin to anarchy'. (2000, 317)

Almost two decades later, tinkhundla was 'resuscitated… as a mechanism by which to restore [Sobhuza II's] … total control of the parliamentary electoral system' (Booth 2000, 318). *Tinkhundla* became the basis for a new electoral system, the *only* legal option, and a very limited one, for engaging in politics. First, in order to participate, one must acquiesce to being a 'loyal subject' – ordinary Swazi 'citizens' are not permitted to participate. Second, candidates for the new parliament had to be either directly appointed by the *ngwenyama* (king) or selected by an electoral college chosen through the *tinkhundla* – thus still effectively accountable only to the king.[3] Under this new *tinkhundla* structure, voting amounted to walking through a gate of a fenced enclosure (kraal) and standing beside the pre-selected candidate one supported! Even then, candidates could only gain public acclamation after having sworn loyalty or allegiance to the chiefs, all of whom were appointed by the king. Clearly, only those who professed loyalty to the king were legally permitted to engage in politics at all.

King Sobhuza II and his supporters claimed the *tinkhundla* system was rooted in Swazi tradition. Indeed, as early as 1955, shortly after the creation of the system, the king gave *tinkhundla* a traditional and cultural spin by describing them as 'royal villages which according to Swazi laws and custom a Swazi King could establish wherever and whenever he wished' (Kuper 1978, 185). However, the system does not appear to have any such roots and existed only in name from the late 1950s until it was revived and fundamentally transformed as part of the broader political changes introduced by the king under the state of emergency. Thus, *tinkhundla* conforms closely to the kind of 'invented tradition' explored by Hobsbawm and Ranger (1983). Indeed, authors such as Hugh Macmillan (1985) and Richard Levin (1991, 1997) have borrowed Hobsbawm and Ranger's framework to analyse *tinkhundla* and other Swazi institutions. Levin, for instance, argues that the systematic process of creating and resuscitating traditions has permitted 'Swazi absolutism' to flourish under a monarchy that is 'far more tenacious than elsewhere in the region' (1997, 2–3). Without such 'invented tradition', the self-serving authoritarianism of the Swazi state would be naked, and therefore much more difficult to defend without using constant and highly visible force.

Despite these legitimating practices, resistance to *tinkhundla* became palpable in the mid-1980s, at the time of Sobhuza II's 1982 death and the political disorder within the royal household that followed (Booth 2000). An underground political movement of ethnic Swazis and Eurafricans, workers, students and university lecturers called the People's United Democratic Movement (PUDEMO) was formed in July 1983. PUDEMO's siSwati name is *Insika Yenkhululeko Yemaswasti*, which translates as 'The Swazi People's Pillar of Freedom' – *insika* is the central pillar that holds up a traditional domed hut in Swaziland (Levin 1997, 195). PUDEMO sought to reclaim Swazi culture through its own use of symbols, attributing 'pillar' to the symbolic and literal meaning of holding up an entire shelter that would be large enough to include multiple approaches towards 'freedom'. PUDEMO's constitution, entitled *The People Shall Govern*, explains the movement's *raison d'être* as 'to unite and mobilise the oppressed majority of the Swazi people against the minority oppressive and exploitative *tinkhundla* rule' (PUDEMO 1983). Its second document, the *People's Manifesto*, created a structure that paralleled the South African ANC's *People's Charter* of 1955, and like the ANC, various factions have developed during PUDEMO's 31-year history. Notably, although PUDEMO calls for the elimination of *tinkhundla* and the establishment of democratic institutions, they have yet to deliberate their position on the continuation or elimination of the monarchy.

In the 1980s, PUDEMO started working clandestinely and distributed pamphlets that called for a return to multi-party democracy. A decade later, the end of apartheid in neighbouring South Africa invigorated PUDEMO, whose criticisms of the *tinkhundla* system as anti-democratic merged with the spirit of change present in southern Africa at that time. Their sustained protests, plus the less hospitable environment for non-democratic political regimes in the developing world, had some effect. In 1991, King Mswati III ordered a review of the electoral system; however, the result was simply a cosmetic reform of procedures. Secret ballot voting was introduced at the second stage of the election, after the candidates had been approved by the king and by voters, who still had to queue behind the one they favoured. The widespread demand for multi-party politics was rejected and the first election under the reformed *tinkhundla* system, held in 1993, confirmed to the voters that the system remained rigged. As Booth notes, the following year saw 'mass labor activism and sporadic political violence' (2000, 318).

A few years later, Mswati III announced the formation a new Constitutional Review Commission (CRC), charged with producing a new constitution within two years. Change was still cosmetic: after the 2003 election, the Commonwealth Expert Team (CET) stated: 'no elections can be credible when they are for a Parliament which does not have power and when political parties are banned' (2003, 18). The constitutional review document was finally released in 2005, leading to some constitutional changes. Notably, however, *tinkhundla* and the no-party system remained intact: '[t]he system of government for Swaziland is a democratic, participatory, *tinkhundla*-based system which emphasises devolution of state power from central government to *tinkhundla* areas' (Government of Swaziland 2005, sect. 79). As we have already seen, *tinkhundla* concentrates power in the king, rather than decentralising it, as implied in the constitution.

Unsurprisingly, even in its new formulation, *tinkhundla* has faced international criticism and opposition groups have made appeals to various international bodies to support deeper democratisation. For example, during the 2008 parliamentary election, both the African Union and Pan-African Parliament urged the Swazi government 'to open a window for political parties to participate in the elections process and further provide funding for candidates to campaign' (Rooney 2008). The Pan-African Parliament pointed out that the restriction on political parties was an infringement on the rights of citizens and did not meet regional or international standards and principles for democratic elections. The 2008 Commonwealth report said much the same, adding that Swaziland needed to look again at its constitution, this time ensuring there was full consultation with the people, civic society and political organisations. The CET went on to say that even under the new 2005 constitution, the election could not be credible:

> The real challenge is to gain the confidence of the democratic dispensation with an entrenched bill of rights, as is expected of Swaziland in accordance with Commonwealth principles and declarations ... We also noted our serious concerns on the inherent inconsistencies and contradictions, particularly as they relate to the separation of powers (or lack thereof) and the rule of law. We also expressed our deep concern for the inconsistency and contradictions as they relate to the interpretation of the fundamental right of freedom of association and assembly, where political parties are denied formal recognition, so that they do not have the right to carry out activities which political parties would normally conduct in a multi-party democracy. (Commonwealth Expert Team 2008, 25)

It is not surprising that international observers all noted the *tinkhundla* parliamentary elections of 2008 lacked credibility; the *tinkhundla* was never designed to be a people-driven democratic institution.

Despite international censure and a growing domestic political opposition movement, the domestic press has been restrained in criticising the government because of extensive media censorship. Swaziland has only one radio station and one television station; both are operated by the government. The king effectively owns one of the two daily newspapers, the *Swazi Observer*, through its investment company, *Tibiyo*. The *Observer* is more a 'praise' paper for the activities of the monarchy and the government than a 'news' paper. The other daily, the *Times of Swaziland*, is owned privately but heavily censored and its operating license is under constant review. Over the past decade, the Media Institute of Southern Africa has noted the lack of free speech and space for dissent. Not surprisingly then, in May 2011 Amnesty International expressed concern over

Swaziland's media being 'restricted by statutory laws and 'sweeping' provisions under the Suppression of Terrorism Act' (Amnesty International 2011).

Tibiyo

The second authoritative institution that has become the focus of popular resistance is *Tibiyo*. The *Tibiyo takaNgwane* Fund was established by Sobhuza II at independence in 1968 and has long been a source of controversy. *Tibiyo takaNgwane*, which literally translates as the 'Wealth of the Swazi Nation', is a royal investment trust. The ownership of Swaziland's natural wealth, specifically its mineral resources, was a significant point of contention among Sobhuza II, the British government and the Swazi opposition parties during the constitutional talks (Baloro 1994). Britain and the newly founded political parties wished to vest Swaziland's mineral wealth in the new parliamentary government, but Sobhuza II wanted it vested in himself, 'in trust for the Swazi nation'. Sobhuza II won, making it possible for the king to make *Tibiyo* his personal source of income and power.

Tibiyo's charter says it promotes the 'material welfare, standard of living and education' of the people, while at the same time preserving their 'customs and traditional institutions' (Booth 2000, 314). *Tibiyo* supporters claim it has continuously promoted the cultural and economic progress of the nation since its inception through agricultural investments, educational scholarships, land repurchase and small business development. In the early years, freehold land was indeed purchased, but much of that land was developed into *Tibiyo*-owned maize and dairy estates. *Tibiyo* also invested in enterprises ranging from butcheries to a state television broadcasting utility, as well as a national airline.

By the 1990s, *Tibiyo* had ceased to be a minerals-based corporation, and had used much of its resources to buy large equity stakes (normally 50% interest) in most of the significant foreign investment ventures in the kingdom. These included investments in asbestos, casinos, construction, food and meat processing, hotels, banks, insurance, sugar and other agribusinesses, mines and timber. Consequently, according to Booth, *Tibiyo* 'has become a principal capital base of the modern Swazi monarchy, [yet] has operated only at the massive cost of skewing national development priorities and draining the central government budget' (2000, 20).

Tibiyo funnels many of its resources to a small elite through patronage and nepotism. Booth clearly identifies the problems with this system and is worth quoting at length:

> The extent to which Tibiyo's resources are invested in the Swazi nation as a whole is unknown because its books are not open to the public. Basically Tibiyo is a closed-end corporation, largely secretive in nature, whose revenues are used in substantial portion to accumulate wealth on behalf of the monarchy and its interests. That is to say that Tibiyo's revenues do not accrue to the Ministry of Finance in Mbabane, but rather to Tibiyo's headquarters in Lozithelezi. Although it is true that a portion of its wealth (there is really no telling how much, although its chairman valued its investments in 1999 at E553million [$88 million]) is also used for the public good, the public arguably pays for much of it by virtue of the fact that Tibiyo is not subject to government taxation. Particularly in the case of Tibiyo, the phrase 'in trust for the Swazi nation' resonates with an especially hollow ring. (2000, 314)

Tibiyo pays no taxes, so while the king uses *Tibiyo* as a personal source of income, 'the national economy benefits only from wages earned and corporate taxes paid (or what is left after *Tibiyo's* exemptions)' (Booth 2000, 20). Further, the government has even turned to international bodies such as the African Development Bank (ADB), World Bank and the International Monetary Fund (IMF) for funds to support *Tibiyo* investments. Swazi citizens will be responsible for repaying these loans through their taxes.

Recently, the IMF expressed concerns about *Tibiyo* after the Swazi government requested a 'letter of comfort' from them verifying the government would be in a position to repay an African Development Bank loan they were requesting. As part of those investigations, in February 2011, Joannes Mongardini, leader of the IMF delegation to Swaziland, called for a review of *Tibiyo's* tax exemption status: 'The status of Tibiyo should be clarified on whether it should be taxable or not. If taxed, Tibiyo would be one of the biggest tax contributors in the country. It is not clear to me why it is not taxed' (W. Dlamini 2011). This comment generated a flurry of nationalist anti-IMF rhetoric; one week later the *Times* reported the minister of finance telling the 'high powered ... IMF delegation to Swaziland to stop interfering' (B. Dlamini 2011). Needless to say, the IMF had been invited in the first place and was just reporting its findings, so the government's response showed the arrogance with which the Swazi monarchy has become accustomed to operating.

Tibiyo's sponsors claim it represents an authentic, pre-colonial, paternalistic form of sovereign governance in the interests of the people, but as we have seen, its practices manifest the modern, authoritarian, acquisitive nature of the Swazi monarchy. The king appoints the governing board that oversees the entire fund and its structures. Although both Sobhuza II and Mswati III have claimed *Tibiyo's* resources are held in trust for the entire nation's benefit, only a very small percentage of the revenues reach the common citizenry. The only way citizens benefit from *Tibiyo* is through university scholarships, most of which are provided to children of the elite. *Tibiyo* also claims to support cultural institutions in the general Swazi interest, but these, too, promote the monarchy's agenda. The operations of *Tibiyo* are opaque, its annual reports are difficult to locate and its official website is no longer functional, meaning there is no accountability for its use of public funds. Apart from sporadic reports in the media about executive appointments, details about board members, duties, salaries, departments, number of employees and so forth are not available.

The picture that emerges from the above discussion is of an increasingly authoritarian regime that uses and manipulates tradition and culture to maintain its grip on society while channelling public funds, including IMF loans, into the king's private accounts. The monarchy defends its actions, in part, by claiming that the country is a 'unique democracy' that cannot be measured against universal standards or international norms. The population is urged to embrace the 'Swazi way', and told rewards will be plentiful for 'traditionalists'. It is true enough that the potential rewards, such as royal appointments or financial allowances, are tangible for those who can and do participate in the *tinkhundla* system, especially for those who are already part of the elite. For example, Mswati III is currently responsible for appointing all local chiefs and *tinkhundla* governors, 20 of the 30 senators, members of the king's council (*liqoqo*), the prime minister and cabinet, as well as the members of the Board of *Tibiyo* and its subsidiary *Tisuka*.[4] Rather than merit, positions are granted for obeisance, and financed by revenues from *Tibiyo*. Thus, while *Tinkhundla* and *Tibiyo* use a discourse of traditionalism to mask the self-serving nature of the monarchy's activities, corruption cements the loyalty of the elite to the Swazi political order.

Resistance and political opposition

Despite the rewards of loyalty and the threat of arrest or other forms of punishment for political dissent, a significant number of Swazis have not been persuaded into becoming the king's 'subjects', and some have expressed their opposition by joining banned political organisations and engaging in other political activities. Those opposed to the king and his rule, especially those who have acted on their opposition, face the considerable coercive power of the state. For example, members of the two main dissident political groups, PUDEMO and its youth wing, Swaziland Youth Congress (SWAYOCO), which advocate for a return to the traditional democracy of multiple parties and parliamentary processes, have been subjected to violence and repression. One prominent instance took place in May 2010, when Sipho Jele wore a PUDEMO t-shirt to the 1 May Workers' Day celebration in Manzini. He was apprehended, taken by police to his homestead where his room was searched and then transported to the Manzini police station for interrogation. Subsequently, he was incarcerated at the Sidwashini Correctional facility, where it was announced three days later that he had committed suicide. The government's autopsy reported nothing unusual about the death, but at the inquest, an independent pathologist from South Africa questioned how Jele could possibly have tied the rope on a shower rod to hang himself when the shower room had neither a chair nor a stool.

The killing of Jele, so reminiscent of events in South Africa during the apartheid era, was intended to terrorise all political activists by reminding them of the coercive power of the Swazi state. Only two years earlier, in 2008, Mswati III had warned the population that such deaths were likely when he commented that those with diverging views from the monarchy would be strangled. At the time, Mswati III's rage was over a bombing near Lozitha Palace two nights after the *tinkhundla* parliamentary elections. This bomb blast was not the first in Swaziland – various structures, such as the parliament building (1996), the *tinkhundla* building (1998), chiefs' homesteads, homes of members of parliament and police stations have been targets. Jabulane Matsebula, PUDEMO representative in Australia, argued that these very strategic bombings threatened the legitimacy of the king:

> Rejected as a yesterday man and a hopeless actor in the global political theatre, King Mswati III returned to home ground [from UN meetings] to vent his anger and frustration on Swazi citizens. Shortly after the United Nations General Assembly, he summoned the nation to his royal residence for what local and international media widely described as a historical event in which the ruling monarch declared war on Swazi and South African citizens. He accused Swazis and South Africans of engaging in acts of terrorism against Swaziland. The rage in his tone and use of sadistic words such as *abakhanywe* (strangle them) generated a deep sense of fear and anxiety in many people. It caused significant concern that a new wave of political repression will soon follow. (PUDEMO 2008)

Despite the danger, civil society organisations such as the Swaziland Coalition of Concerned Civic Organisations, unions and banned political opposition parties and groups have exerted ongoing pressure on the monarchy. Their growing activism has been fuelled by the predatory nature of the Swazi elite, who have continued to plunder the nation's resources while remaining 'specialist in violence' (Bates 2008, 7).

Although the state has responded to growing opposition, including public displays of dissidence through songs, with violence and oppression, until recently it has stopped short of intervening in highly personal events like vigils and funerals, even when they were for political activists. Recently, however, it has attempted to limit or ban funerals or to prevent singing at such funerals of political activists. This strategy may prove effective in shutting down one further avenue for expressing dissent, but taking such a dramatic step as to ban funerals, an important site of culture and tradition, instead may force the state's hand into the open. It will be more difficult than ever to claim to be upholding tradition when the police and military are invading one of the most basic traditions of the country, the opportunity for family and friends to bury a loved one and grieve together. And it is this difficulty that the political opposition is counting on as it continues to use songs and traditional music at funerals to challenge the regime – 're-claiming' culture and tradition to push for 'modern' political reforms.

Songs and funerals

Music and song have long been used in politics. We need look no further than to neighbouring South Africa, where both were used effectively throughout the liberation struggle against the apartheid regime. In a society characterised by censorship and state control, coupled with significant social tensions, music can become both a safe haven and a centre of controversial discourse (Byerly 1998, 36). Political songs act as social commentaries, expressing stinging critiques aimed at the government. The lyrics of protest songs can threaten the state, or endanger 'the whole fabric of society' as Plato once noted, and there is a long history of songs of political significance or influence in southern Africa. The importance of political songs in anti-colonial and anti-apartheid struggles has not been well researched, perhaps because they belong to an oral rather than a written tradition. Most songs are not attributed to an individual, but thought of as collective compositions that are altered according to the historical or local context.

This section argues that within the oppressive atmosphere of Swaziland, protest music has become one of the most important ways to express political dissent because other spaces for open resistance have been 'strangled out'. Moreover, protest songs are not costly to distribute, less dangerous to store and easier to transmit (given there may be illiteracy in rural areas) than printed pamphlets. The songs discussed in this article were recorded in Swaziland in 2008. Most were sung by members of PUDEMO and SWAYOCO at the memorial service and funeral of lawyer and political activist Musa J. Dlamini.[5] It should be noted that these songs may not be entirely representative of the genre of protest music in Swaziland because the music analysed here is not based on an anthology of songs from various occasions and time periods (such as meetings or street demonstrations); such an anthology of protest music in Swaziland is simply lacking due to the hostile political environment. What this collection does highlight is several significant features of protest in song in Swaziland.

Freedom or struggle songs in Swaziland act as a musical counterpoint to the dominant and static notion of culture defined by the monarchy. Whereas the monarchy asserts a purity and singularity to Swazi culture, this collection of songs represents a counter-culture that situates Swazis within a southern African context. Rather than a purely inward looking Swazi view, these songs reflect an adaptable, outward looking cultural perspective, reflecting a greater commonality with and fluidity among the various Nguni cultures of southern Africa.

The songs in this collection contain a tone of defiance rather than supplication. Unlike songs from South Africa such as *Senzenina* (What have we done) and *Thinasizwe* (We African people), which are characterised by a self-reflective tone and sense of despair, these songs avoid any sense of powerlessness or hopelessness. Their outlook is combatant, positive and affirmative with a sense of urgency and agency. None of the Swazi songs discussed here actually question why people were faced with challenges and struggles, but rather emphasised their refusal to accept the current situation and their resistance to its perceived injustice.

The song structure is a 'call and response' and the melody usually remains constant when the song travels, while the lyrics can be spontaneously improvised.[6] All the songs are composed of a short phrase, verse or slogan that is continuously sung as a chant: two or four eight-beat phrases that are repeated. The lyrics of these resistance songs are predominantly siSwati with some English words used occasionally. With only minimal lyrics, it is difficult to allocate the term 'narrative' to any specific song, but when gathered collectively, they provide distilled images of importance. These historical snapshots, or struggle soundscapes, then become part of a collage that tells a 'history from below'. Two songs that provide historical snapshots are *Marshall Law* and *You were not there*.

> *Marshall Law*
> Living under Marhsall Law
> State of Emergency
> We're living under Marshall
> State of Emergency
> *You were not there*
> were not there
> when we hit parliament.
> You were not there
> when they arrested.
> The gun going para! parah!

The first song alludes to the 1973 decree, reminding the listener that the people are still living under a state of emergency. The second song prompts the listener to remember the events of 1994, when the first unquestionably overt act of sabotage, the bombing of the parliament, took place. For the resistance movement, continually reminding people of the repressive acts of the state – and informing those who might not know or might be willing to forget – is important to build and maintain support for the movement. Songs offer one of the few outlets to do so.

The songs also capture personal experience. The lyrics are focused on the difficulties of the political struggle, but these issues are broad enough to be felt by a large segment of society and therefore representative of the daily struggle in Swaziland. Where unemployment (40% prior to the global recession of 2008), poverty (70% living on less than $1 per day), domestic violence and HIV/AIDS have contributed to the extremely harsh socio-economic situation, many can identify with the message in the songs:

> We're struggling
> under hard conditions
> we got arrested

beaten
no food
no drugs/medicine
and struggling under hard conditions.

Such experiences are not narrated through codes designed to evade the censors – the language is direct and the meaning explicit. The simple and straightforward words link the struggles of the movement to those of the entire community. The upbeat tempo signals resilience rather than victimisation; the implied message is 'we will not give up'. Other songs talk of solutions, and the language is direct with the lyrics literally calling on the guerillas to defend the people. All these songs exhibit a tone of unambiguous defiance and noncompliance rather than acquiescence.

Some of the songs refer directly to SWAPLA, the Swaziland People's Liberation Army. In August 2008, one month prior to national elections and the lavish '40–40' king's birthday/independence celebrations, SWAPLA announced their formation in a press statement. This song speaks of a Swazi liberation army preparing its soldiers, the people; its lyrics focus on arming civilians and teaching people how to defend themselves – the young and the old are both accepted in the people's army. AKA refers to an AK 47:

SWAPLA takes young boys
gives them AKA
SWAPLA takes old women
teaches them how to use AKA
SWAPLA takes old people
teaches them how to use AKA
SWAPLA for the nation.

These songs advocate a far more intensive form of militancy than earlier resistance songs of the 1980s or 1990s, which were characterised by lyrics like 'we are marching for multi-party democracy'. This may indicate that although the monarchy still describes Swaziland as a 'peaceful kingdom' (one of a maze of euphemisms), the younger generations now interpret this apparent 'peacefulness' as being silenced and beaten, and are fighting back and calling on people to join in this resistance.

The lyrics are also used to build morale amongst the singers and community. Songs air grievances, identify the oppressor, sometimes mock or ridicule them, and point to a way forward. *Icalalalo* alludes to land evictions, where land was appropriated without compensation for *Tibiyo* investment projects, and other crimes against the people:

Icalalalabo
Solo: Their crimes
Response: Their crimes
Solo: Their crimes
Response: Their crimes are so big
So bring us the guns
So big is the crime
So they can speak
So you will speak
Our homes are being destroyed
Bring us the guns

This song is equally focused on 'their crimes' and the people's resolute conviction to resist. It represents a drastic transition from being a loyal and peaceful 'subject' of the king to becoming an agent of one's own destiny; it reflects a shift in consciousness. The people's resolve is represented as a response to 'their crimes', in the sense of self-defence rather than aggression or anger. Implicit in the text is the idea that the people have been forced to take action, forced to defend themselves and their communities, and therefore forced to engage in armed struggle. Performed slower than a walking pace, the tempo of this song drags without joy or energy like a slow funeral march. It offers a sorrowful and solemn resolve to take action rather than the jubilant determination of an eager combatant.

Both the lyrics and the musical form of the compositions are equally significant cultural statements that represent clear alternatives to official culture as practised and promoted by the king. Resistance songs have the qualities that characterise music (melody, rhythm, harmony, timbre, expression and form) and generally praise 'the people' rather than the king. The majority of resistance songs are in the form of 'call and response' where one singer acts as the initiator of the song and the collective responds simultaneously. The leader and chorus echo back and forth in a mutual exchange, a dialogue that can express and engage a multitude of diverse voices simultaneously, and although an individual person 'leads', the leaders, or callers, rotate from one individual to another, democratising the musical form to symbolically represent the act of democratising the political leadership. In this way, the dialogue becomes part of a 'social language' marked by 'shared knowledge' and 'cultural commonality' (Gunner 2009, 330).

The 'call and response' form can be contrasted to the traditional style of the *ibizonga* (praise singer). In Swaziland, as well as other southern African nations, the *ibizonga* is a male poet who walks ahead of the king and recites verses that highlight his positive traits. The *ibizonga* is employed at the royal court and works individually to create and recite these verses at ceremonial occasions. There is no melody, and certainly no audience participation, involved in these 'praise songs' and they are more reminiscent of a recitation rather than a conventional song. In contrast, the fluidity and interactive nature of resistance songs reveals their political underpinnings as a collective project, which is symbolically important in a society dominated by the monologue of the king's *ibizonga*.

Political funerals

Scholars have noted 'political funerals are especially likely to arise in societies where modernisation coincides with highly repressive political systems' (Goldstein 1984, 16). In this section, I explain that until recently, funerals remained one of the very last 'free sites' for political expression in Swaziland. Draconian laws were, however, introduced immediately after the funeral of M.J. Dlamini, at whose funeral the songs in this article were recorded, in an attempt to shut down one of the few remaining spaces for political dissent. The capacity of the state to close down funerals as sites of political dissent and, if successful, the implications for the resistance movement were not known at the time of writing, nor were the implications for the state itself, which necessarily has made its repressive capacity more visible than ever by invading private spaces to an extent beyond that seen in the past by seeking to police funerals.

Previous attempts to depoliticise funerals in Swaziland usually involved threatening the family of the deceased, whose occupancy on family farms could be endangered by overt political statements at funerals. From time to time, newspapers reported of clashes between the family and political organisations when political activists died. For example, in 'Late Mashaya's funeral turned political rally', the *Times* reported that 'political parties' members hijacked the funeral' and the family and pastor 'were left shocked' (Mathunjwa and Sizwe 2009).[7] After M.J. Dlamini's funeral, the *Times* reported that Dlamini's parents were called to the local chief's kraal to apologise for their son's actions or face eviction, not only from their land but also from the country. Such threats against the families of political activists were intended to send a message to political activists to temper their activities at funerals, or else risk endangering the family, which would further isolate activists from the community.

The funeral of M.J. Dlamini marked the first time the state responded overtly to what was said at a funeral. At his memorial and funeral, struggle songs were interspersed with prayers and speeches: generally one song followed by one speaker. When the speaker was a family or church member, the gathering sang a Christian hymn; when the speaker was a friend, political activist or union representative, a struggle song would begin. Because these gatherings have 'religious and sacred overtones' that make it 'highly inadvisable to interfere' (Goldstein 1984, 17), the state did not disrupt the vigil or funeral. But they responded within a few weeks by introducing the Suppression of Terrorism Act, which was legislated in November 2008. Two days later, they used their new powers to arrest PUDEMO's president, Mario Masuku, using as evidence recordings police said they had made at M.J. Dlamini's funeral where he was alleged to have made terrorist remarks. He remained in prison for 10 months while his trial was continually postponed, but in September 2009, Judge Mamba ended the trial in four hours because of the weakness of the prosecution's case. Many who attended the funeral said Masuku was guilty of nothing and the charges were false.

Nontheless, in proceeding with the charges, the state still had made its point. By the time of the funeral of Sipho Jele, another political activist whose suspicious death was mentioned above, funerals had become a policed space and the state attempted to silence the music. Political activists in attendance estimated that more than 500 police were present, completely surrounding the entire ground. Police interrupted the Friday vigil, trying to stop struggle songs and political speeches. The burial was disrupted in the morning and Jele's body had to be returned to the mortuary. The following weekend, the Royal Police enforced a no PUDEMO t-shirt mandate and interrupted political songs and speeches but did allow the body to be buried. Student activist Pius Vilakati defiantly wore a PUDEMO t-shirt and had to be smuggled away from the funeral by hiding in the hearse. He has since gone into political exile in South Africa, where he is active with Swaziland Solidarity Network.

The long term implications of the state's efforts to shut down political dissent at funerals were not yet clear at the time of writing. If the state is able to succeed in closing down one more place of dissent, the monarchy may be able to restabilise their rule for a few more months or years. But openly interrupting the vigil and funeral site makes the state's motives clear – it would be difficult to explain these actions as upholding Swazi tradition, though undoubtedly, some effort will be made to claim to be protecting the family of the deceased. If such legitimating efforts fail, the state's naked use of power will be visible to a large portion of the Swazi population, which may ultimately undermine their authority. Even if they succeed, and if history is any guide to the future, closing funerals as sites of resistance will not silence dissent in Swaziland, but merely redirect it to new spaces where it can burst forth in song.

Conclusion

This article has shown that the contested categories of 'culture' and 'tradition' in Swaziland are the product of, on the one hand, colonialist, neocolonialist and now imperialist intonations; and, on the other hand, the Swazi royal family's adaptation and manipulation of culture and tradition to gain legitimacy. Dating back to the anti-colonial struggle, the Swazi monarchy used 'tradition' to legitimate its right to rule both with the colonial power, Britain, and with Swazis. By the 1960s, fledging political parties refused the notion of 'tribal nationalism' implied in Sobhuza II's depiction of Swazi tradition and sought instead a pluralist society. Yet the fixed motif of tribal culture was sufficiently compelling to enable a dominant group, the Dlamini monarchy, to grasp power and portray itself as the only valid, legitimate authority in Swaziland. Institutions designed to maintain their power, like *tinkhundla* and *tibiyo*, were justified by reference to ancient Swazi traditions, when in fact, as Macmillan (1985) and Levin (1991, 1997) have shown, their actual history conforms more closely to Hobsbawm and Ranger's (1983) notion of 'invented tradition'.

The resistance examined in this article is primarily directed towards the political repression and naked greed of Swaziland's monarchy, but has taken the route of contesting the monarchy's static definition of culture and the institutions that impose this culture. Too often, the facade of culture and tradition has dulled people's analytical powers (Said 1993, 191) and many Swazis accepted the mythical Swaziland, 'valley of heaven', as the African Switzerland. Yet, culture is not static, it is multi-dimensional and multi-local and many Swazis resist the tribal nationalism that has been forced upon them. They refuse to be dictated to and prefer their own definition of what it means to be Swazi. Increasingly, they are rejecting and resisting the monarchy's monopoly on culture as well as its monopoly on politics and violence, propelling this living African museum, Mswati III's farm, into the twenty-first century.

Notes

1. *Ngwenyama* literally means 'lion'. During colonial times, the British translated this term as 'Paramount Chief' because they would only permit one monarch within the empire and that was the king/queen of England. Moreover, as Paramount Chief, the *Ngwenyama's* authority extended only to ethnic Swazis, not to the white settlers or those of mixed race (Baloro 1994, 20–21).
2. The INM won 85.45% of the vote in the June 1964 election (and all the seats), with the balance of the votes – 12.3% – going to the NNLC.
3. Any member of the public who wishes to enter politics must first swear allegiance, *kukhonta*, to a local chief, and then be given royal assent before becoming a candidate.
4. It is not unusual to see a member of the royal family shifted from one position to another. For example, in October 2008, Prime Minister Themba Dlamini was removed as the head of the government and transferred to the position of Managing Director of *Tibiyo*, a position he had previously held before he was appointed as prime minister.
5. The songs were translated from siSwati to English by Mq. Nxumalo in October and November 2008 in Manzini, Swaziland. M.J. Dlamini was a founding member of Lawyers for Human Rights and the National Constitutional Assembly. Although never an open proponent of armed struggle, police allege he died when planting a bomb at Lozitha Bridge. According to several sources, after many years practising law in Swaziland, he realised the immobility of the

monarchy's position on democratic reforms and may have participated in acts of sabotage (field notes and personal communication).

6. Lyrics could be considered extra-musical because they do not fall strictly within one of the six elements of music, which are melody, harmony, rhythm, timbre, form and expression. However, lyrics in combination with melody contribute to the expression of a song, because lyrics give music the unique ability 'to carry information and political messages' that are otherwise silenced and suppressed in media and society (Byerly 1998, 31).

7. It is possible this family was unaware or disapproved of their son's political beliefs and activities, but in any case, they would be unable to show open acceptance of these political activities at the funeral, because doing so can put the family's home and property at risk.

References

Amnesty International. 2011. *Amnesty International Report 2011 – Swaziland*. Accessed June 21. http://www.amnesty.org/en/region/swaziland/report-2011.

Ayee, Joseph. 1989. "A Note on the Machinery of Government during the Sobhuza II Era in Swaziland." *Institute of African Studies Research Review* 5 (1): 54–68.

Baloro, John M. 1994. "The Development of Swaziland's Constitution: Monarchical Responses to Modern Challenges." *Journal of African Law* 38 (1): 19–34. doi:10.1017/S0021855300011438.

Bates, Robert H. 2008. *When Things Fell Apart: State Failure in Late-Century Africa*. New York: Cambridge University Press.

Booth, Alan R. 2000. *A Historical Dictionary*. Lanham: Scarecrow Press.

Byerly, Ingrid Bianca. 1998. "Mirror, Mediator, and Prophet: The Music Indaba of Late-Apartheid South Africa." *Ethnomusicology* 42 (1): 1–44. doi:10.2307/852825.

Commonwealth Expert Team. 2003. *Swaziland National Elections*. Accessed July 25, 2011. http://www.thecommonwealth.org/shared_asp_files/uploadedfiles/%7B9C9C4FF0-8E15-40E4-98B1-38FE7A81FF9%7D_SwazilandNationalElections_report.pdf.

Commonwealth Expert Team. 2008. *Swaziland National Elections*. Accessed August 5, 2011. http://www.thecommonwealth.org/files/184644/FileName/SwazilandNationalElections2008-CETReportFinalPrint.pdf.

Dlamini, Banele. 2011. "IMF Called to Order." *Times of Swaziland*, March 4. Accessed May 5, 2011. http://www.times.co.sz/news/62433-imf-called-to-order.html.

Dlamini, Welcome. 2011. "Consider Taxing Tibiyo – IMF." *Times of Swaziland*, February 28, 2011. Accessed March 7, 2011. http://www.times.co.sz/news/62335-consider-taxing-tibiyo-%C3%A2%E2%82%AC%E2%80%9D-imf.html.

Goldstein, Robert Justin. 1984. "Political Funerals." *Society* 21 (3): 13–17. doi:10.1007/BF02700363.

Government of Swaziland. 2005. *The Constitution of the Kingdom of Swaziland Act, 2005*. Accessed November 23, 2010. http://www.gov.sz/images/stories/Constitution%20of%20%20SD-2005A001.pdf.

Grotpeter, John J. 1975. *Historical Dictionary of Swaziland*. Metuchen, NJ: Scarecrow Press.

Gunner, Liz. 2009. "Jacob Zuma, the Social Body and the Unruly Power of Song." *African Affairs* 108 (430): 27–48. doi:10.1093/afraf/adn064.

Hobsbawm, Eric, and Terence Ranger, eds. 1983. *The Invention of Tradition*. Cambridge: Cambridge University Press.

Jackson, Robert H., and Carl G. Rosberg. 1982. *Personal Rule in Black Africa*. Berkeley: University of California Press.

Kuper, Hilda. 1978. *Sobhuza II*. London: Duckworth.

Levin, Richard. 1991. "Swaziland's Tinkhundla and the Myth of Swazi tradition." *Journal of Contemporary African Studies* 10 (2): 1–23. doi:10.1080/02589009108729511.

Levin, Richard. 1997. *When the Sleeping Grass Awakens*. Johannesburg: Witwatersrand University Press.

Lewis, Stephen. 2005. *Race against Time*. Toronto: House of Anansi Press.

Macmillan, Hugh. 1985. "Swaziland: Decolonisation and the Triumph of 'Tradition'." *Journal of Modern African Studies* 23 (4): 643–666. doi:10.1017/S0022278X00055014.

Mathunjwa, Nhlanhla, and Sizwe. 2009. "Late Mashaya's Funeral Turned into Political Rally." *Times of Swaziland*, May 18, 2009. Accessed September 9. http://www.times.co.sz/news/2546-late-mashaya-s-funeral-turned-into-political-rally.html.

Potholm, Christian. 1972. *Swaziland*. Berkeley: University of California Press.

PUDEMO (People's United Democratic Movement) 1983. *PUDEMO Constitution: The People Shall Govern*. Accessed August 5, 2011. http://www.pudemo.org/Docs/People%20constitution.pdf.

PUDEMO (People's United Democratic Movement) 2008. *Strangling the King's Opponents: Swaziland's 'War on Terrorism.'* http://swazilandsolidaritynetworkcanada.wikispaces.com/Strangling+the+King%E2%80%99s+opponents++Swaziland%E2%80%99s+%E2%80%9Cwar+on+terrorism%E2%80%9D+Nov+24%2C+2008.

"Republic of South Africa." 2008. *Mail & Guardian*, December 9. Accessed September 7, 2009. www.mg.co.za.

Rooney, Richard. 2008. "Poll Observers Want Parties". Accessed May 27, 2010. http://swazielections.blogspot.ca/2008/09/poll-observers-want-parties.html.

Said, Edward. 1993. *Culture and Imperialism*. New York: Knopf.

SIPA (Swaziland Investment Promotion Authority) 2008. *Swaziland Business Year Book*. 17th ed., edited by Christina Forsyth Thompson. Mbabane: SIPA.

Stevens, R. P. 1963. "Swaziland Political Development". *Journal of Modern African Studies* 1 (3): 327–350. doi:10.1017/S0022278X00001737.

Vieceli, Jackie. 1982. "Swaziland after Sobhuza: Stability or Crisis?" *Issue: A Journal of Opinion* 12 (3/4): 56–63. doi:10.2307/1166718.

The Zimbabwean People's Army moment in Zimbabwean history, 1975–1977: Mugabe's rise and democracy's demise

David Moore

Department of Anthropology and Development Studies, University of Johannesburg, Johannesburg, South Africa

This article provides a historical analysis of Robert Mugabe's rise to power in the fractious hierarchy of the Zimbabwe African National Union (ZANU), in part by crushing all opposition and manipulating regional and international actors – including British, American and Mozambican political leaders – into supporting his claims to leadership. It also tells an often-ignored story of internal political struggle during the liberation war involving a small group of young political soldiers, the Zimbabwean People's Army (ZIPA), which challenged the policies, practices and ideology of the 'old guard' and tried to unify ZANU and Zimbabwe African People's Union, the country's two nationalist movements at the time. Drawing on interviews and extensive archival data, the article argues that ideology was central to this political struggle; ZIPA embraced a more radical and potentially more democratic vision for the liberation movement and for the future of the country. What kind of regime might have been consolidated in post-independent Zimbabwe if ZIPA had succeeded in unifying the country's national liberation movement and pushing them into the political direction ZIPA desired? This will never be known. By 1977, less than two years after the group emerged, its leaders were imprisoned in Mozambique's jails where they would remain until just prior to Zimbabwe's first democratic election in 1980.

Much of Zimbabwe's liberation war history is unknown. Of that which is known, much is misunderstood. These lacunae make it harder to comprehend the country's contemporary crisis clearly. In this article, I argue that to grasp Zimbabwe's liberation history properly, it is helpful to look back to the rise and demise of a small group of young and radical political soldiers, the Zimbabwean People's Army (ZIPA), who took the war of liberation out of its deep lull mid-1970s by articulating a profound critique of the political and ideological tendencies of Zimbabwe's nationalist 'old guard' (Ranger 1980). This allowed them to make real progress towards unifying Zimbabwe's two most important nationalist parties. Yet they were removed from the scene summarily by Robert Mugabe, with the assistance of Mozambique's president Samora Machel, and incarcerated for over three years.

The brief but intense history of ZIPA is not merely of intrinsic interest (Mhanda 2011; Moore 1991, 1995). It illuminates some of the ways in which Robert Mugabe rose to the top of the Zimbabwe African National Union's[1] (ZANU) fractious hierarchy. Also, it shows how 'western' forces – decades later condemned by Robert Mugabe as evil imperialists – assisted Mugabe in removing ZIPA and thus helped him become ZANU's leader. Sophisticated political examination, exemplified by John Saul's intervention on ZIPA (Saul 1979), can expose many of the contours and tendencies within complex global, generational and ideological levels of analysis, but such careful study is rare. The sediments waiting buried in the archives confirm only the best of the political genre. Thus, this essay also serves as an archival verification of Saul's conjunctural analysis, which saw ZIPA about to be sacrificed to American Secretary of State Henry Kissinger's cold war fears. More than three decades after the fact, Saul held his 1977 examination of the 'ZIPA moment' as an indication of his distance from Robert Mugabe's style of rule, labelled 'a very evil outcome indeed', then and now (Saul 2010, 105, 160). In contrast, ZIPA's 'genuinely revolutionary impulse' served as a beacon for Saul's ideas of socialism in Africa (1979, 111). Both the positive and the negative dimensions of Southern Africa's 'liberation legacy', then, are encompassed in ZIPA's flowering and crushing (Trewhela 2009; Leys and Saul 1995).

The context

What Masipula Sithole (1979) called 'struggles within the struggle' were a constituent part of Zimbabwe's long and arduous path towards national liberation. They went far beyond ethnic bases of tension to include ideology, generation, regional affiliation, strategy and even, simply, personality clashes. In 1963, the nationalist movement, the Zimbabwean African People's Union (ZAPU), split when Ndabaningi Sithole formed ZANU.[2] In 1971, ZAPU fell to pieces due to ethnic, generational and ideological disputes (Tshabangu 1979). In March 1975, ZANU's Lusaka (Zambia)-based national chairman, Herbert Chitepo, was killed when his Volkswagen exploded (White 2003). Even after majority rule in 1980, ZANU-Patriotic Front (PF) launched *Gukurahundi* ('the first rain which washes away the chaff before the spring storms'), in which approximately 20,000 residents of Matabeleland and the Midlands were killed in order to eliminate ZAPU under the guise of dealing with a few hundred 'dissidents' (Catholic Commission for Justice and Peace and the Legal Resources Foundation [1997] 2008; Phimister 2008).

Given this history, it should not be surprising that Zimbabwe's rulers resorted to violence and electoral fraud when confronted with a popular opposition party like the Movement for Democratic Change (MDC). The MDC has been cheated out of legitimate power since its first election contest in 2000 (Moore and Raftopoulos 2012). By 2009, the MDC was an unhappy partner in a 'government of national unity' cobbled together by the Southern African Development Community (with South Africa's then-President Thabo Mbeki as 'facilitator' of the solution) in recognition of ZANU-PF's inability to abide by the 2008 election results that awarded the MDC parliamentary victory (Booysen 2009; EISA 2008). Even with its life in power extended, indeed, strengthened by the discovery of huge diamond reserves, ZANU-PF's internal friction sharpened towards its 30th year and even into its 35th, bolstered by its 'victory' in the 2103 elections accepted by the relevant powers (Moore 2014a, 2014b) at the helm of Zimbabwe (Saunders 2010, 2014).

Although the origins of these conflicts were (and are) internally generated, they were inextricably intertwined with regional and international tensions, most notably the cold war (Onslow 2009). When it became clear that ZAPU was developing close relations with the Soviet Union, the USA became interested in helping alternative movements (Moore 2005, 2008). When the Portuguese coup left Angola and Mozambique open to the 'Marxist–Leninist' leadership of Agostinho Neto's Movement for the Popular Liberation of Angola and Samora Machel's Front for the Liberation of Mozambique, the regional and international dimensions of the Zimbabwean struggle took on added dimensions. South Africa feared Zimbabwe would be the next domino to fall, a fear shared by the Americans (less so the British, at least under the Labour Party). Within the region, differences of opinion between Tanzanian president Julius Nyerere and his Zambian counterpart Kenneth Kaunda also helped shape the formation of ZANU.

Given all these fissures and fractions, one might ask: what was so special about ZIPA? As the following pages will illustrate, first, this 'struggle within the struggle' revived the flagging liberation war. Second, ZIPA came close to putting the nationalist movement back together after nearly a decade and a half of separation. Third, the sort of leftism that core constituents of ZIPA initiated involved a creative fusion of Soviet and Chinese tendencies. Fourth, and perhaps most importantly, the young soldier-politicians in ZIPA were the first to recognise the negative traits in Robert Mugabe's style of rule. Ironically, their part in deposing ZANU president Ndabaningi Sithole after he blatantly sided with those promoting the 1974 détente with the white regime, which would have left far too much power with Rhodesian President Ian Smith, contributed significantly to Mugabe's rise.

ZIPA: a brief history

Before examining ZIPA's archival traces, an outline of its saga is necessary. Twelve years after its 1963 split, ZANU appeared to be in ruins. When its leaders were released from Rhodesian prisons at the end of 1974 to participate in a Zambian and South African inspired 'détente' exercise, none of the statesmen along Zimbabwe's front lines or further afield knew if ZANU's president was Ndabaningi Sithole (who had been leader since May 1964) or Robert Mugabe, who had apparently replaced him in a 'coup in prison' (Martin and Johnson 1980, 150). Many new parties emerged, trying to attain seats around the imagined table to negotiate a new dispensation in Rhodesia. In early 1975, rebellions in ZANU's army, the Zimbabwean African National Liberation Army (ZANLA), had spread to Lusaka, where they were quelled by the stern hand of ZANLA's commander, Josiah Tongogara. When ZANU's leader-in-exile, Herbert Chitepo, was assassinated on 17 March 1975, the Zambian state imprisoned the suspects, including Tongogara, and ZANLA's approximately 1500 soldiers were corralled in their camps.

The young military commanders who would become ZIPA were extremely disappointed with Ndabaningi Sithole's minimal efforts to assist their comrades-in-arms arrested for killing Chitepo. They organised resistance among the detainees, but when the Zambians and other enemies got too close they escaped the carnage to negotiate restarting the war with Julius Nyerere, who was both President of Tanzania and director of the Organisation of African Unity's Liberation Committee. On their way they stopped at the Mgagao training camp in Tanzania. There, with more than 40 other ZANLA commanders, they drafted the Mgagao Declaration. It stated they would restart the war with a unified army, that ZANU's president Ndabaningi Sithole had discredited himself, and that the 'next in line', Robert Mugabe (who was an entity unknown to the soldiers but just below Sithole in the party's hierarchy) should step in (Mgagao Declaration,[3] October 1975; cited in Baumhögger 1984 and in Chung 2006, 340–346). Their next stop was Nyerere's office, where they convinced him they were legitimate.

By November 1975, ZIPA started the liberation war anew with a High Command composed of one-half former commanders of the Zimbabwe People's Revolutionary Army (ZIPRA), which was ZAPU's armed wing, with the other 50% formerly from ZANLA (ZANU). The new generation of commanders in ZIPA – often labelled the *vashandi* ('workers' or 'the people') – portended a new, Marxist-inspired radicalism that had the potential to take the nationalist movement in a new direction. Its *de facto* leader, Dzinashe Machingura, was Deputy Political Commissar. His ideological comrades made up more than a third of the 18 member High Command. They did most of ZIPA's work and thus had disproportionate power.

By early 1976, ZIPA had more than 2000 recruits, including 500 from ZIPRA. As Mhanda recalls, young Zimbabweans were 'flooding in due to the collapse of the Portuguese regime. We didn't have to recruit because strictly speaking these people were waiting in the refugee camps'. Indeed, the influx had to be slowed beginning in August 1976 (Mhanda 2011). Of the guerrilla soldiers, more than 1600 were deployed in Rhodesia and by March 1976 the British newspapers were full of stories attesting to ZIPA's actions (Moore 1990, 329, 344). The *vashandi* core of ZIPA developed ideological resources to train a new leadership corps, with radical notions of democratising the military and media strategies of its own, as well as beginning to delegate representatives abroad. Tanzania's media began to refer to the new army as a 'third force' representing an alternative to the old brand of Zimbabwean nationalists.

There were three types of response to this new venture. First, the Rhodesian forces responded with more brutal force than ever, including attacks on refugee camps in Mozambique that killed thousands. Second, international forces (represented by Henry Kissinger) increased pressure on Smith (through the South African Prime Minister John Vorster) to give up his dream of ruling for 1000 years and instead allow moderate black nationalists to share political power. British Foreign Secretary Anthony Crosland and Henry Kissinger co-operated to organise a conference in Geneva for late 1976 to get a new regime on track (Onslow 2006). ZIPA's radical elements resisted, especially because they were expected to line-up behind one leader instead of participating as a united front (*Daily News* [Tanzania], 1, 4, 8, 9 October 1976). They were forced, eventually, to attend.

Third, Robert Mugabe, who moved to Mozambique in order to take control of the guerrilla forces, but was delayed by being incarcerated under house arrest by the Mozambican state, managed to persuade the 'west' that he controlled the guerrilla soldiers making such impressive forays. This began in January 1976, when he persuaded Mozambique's President Machel to allow him to leave the house to visit his apparently ailing wife in a London hospital. The British Broadcasting Corporation (BBC) interviewed him there, and his claims that the guerrilla soldiers were loyal to him were soon broadcast internationally. He also met sympathetic representatives of the British state – one of whom had been looking after his wife since 1967 (Martin and Johnson 1980, 209; Smith and Simpson 1981, 94; Moore 2005).

Training camp disputes in June 1976 between former ZIPRA and former ZANLA soldiers later resulted in casualties. ZAPU withdrew its soldiers, claiming a Chinese and Tanzanian conspiracy to eliminate them, and all but one of the ZAPU contingent of the leadership left (77 cadres of the African National Council (Zimbabwe), Morogoro Camp 1976). This made ZIPA appear little more than a component of ZANU, but ZIPA's effective leadership retained the idea of unity, refusing to identify itself with Mugabe alone. However, by the time of the Geneva conference in October, Mugabe had gone a long way towards persuading the important interlocutors that he was in control of the ZIPA soldiers, even though they were refusing to go to the conference. Simultaneous with the beginning of the conference, the imprisoned ZANU leaders accused of killing Chitepo were released (ostensibly because the evidence against them had been obtained under torture) and sent to Mozambique. There, they joined forces with Mugabe, and, with Machel's assistance, forced the reluctant ZIPA cadres to attend the conference with the ZANU delegation (although, partially following one of the ZIPA commanders' recommendations, Mugabe did agree to form a united front with Joshua Nkomo and ZAPU at a political, not military level; this was the beginning of the 'Patriotic Front' – see footnote 1).

On returning to Mozambique for the Christmas recess (from which the conference was never to reconvene), the radical guerrilla leaders were accused of planning a coup and imprisoned in Mozambique's jails. Later, they would be placed in prison camps in Mozambique's far north. Mugabe had managed to stitch together an alliance of politicians inside Rhodesia, international exiles and members within the military wings of the party while in Geneva; this he consolidated within a few months through the imposition of a new central committee. At its inaugural meeting in July 1977, the new leader warned those thinking of pursuing a *vashandi* agenda: 'When we find it no longer possible to persuade them into the harmony that binds us all ... the ZANU axe' will 'continue to fall' on their necks (Mugabe 1977). The *vashandi* component of ZIPA remained incarcerated by Mozambique until just before Zimbabwe's 1980 election. At ZANU-PF's second congress in August 1984 – the first having been 20 years prior – Mugabe denounced the 'Dzino revolt' (after Dzinashe Machingura, ZIPA's *de facto* leader) as the work of 'treacherous ... counter-revolutionary elements [and] trouble-makers' (Mugabe 1985).

Many contend that ZIPA is little more than a footnote in Zimbabwe's history, affirming the 'official' contention that the *vashandi* movement was simply an 'ultra-leftist' component within an essentially ZANU project (Astrow 1983; Mandaza 1986; Ndlovu-Gatsheni 2009; Martin and Johnson 1980). A few works, following Saul, took the ZIPA radicals more seriously (Moore 1990, 1991, 1995; O'Brien 2009). The evidence to date of ZIPA's fate demonstrates it was a 'real' challenge both to the Zimbabwean nationalist movement's 'petty-bourgeois' leadership and to American foreign policy-makers. It was something approaching a 'revolution within the revolution', analogous to the similar process in ZAPU (Tshabangu 1979). It is churlish to write ZIPA off as yet another strain of 'petty-bourgeois nationalism', as did Astrow's *Zimbabwe: A Revolution that Lost Its Way?* (1983), or to think it was important only for western 'romantic leftists' imposing their scholarly hegemony over African political studies (Mandaza 1986). Memoirs and biographies emerging from the participants in the Zimbabwean struggle confirm ZIPA's unique nature, if sometimes obliquely and with differing degrees of accuracy (Bhebe 2004; Chung 2006; Tekere 2007).

In what follows, I will indicate the ways in which representatives of 'the west' interpreted the ZIPA moment, and Mugabe's role within it, through British and American archival traces and some interviews. They show that concerns with cold war politics, 'tribalist' interpretations of Zimbabwean politics, and hasty efforts to find a 'moderate' leader capable of controlling the 'radicals' and restraining the USSR's influence helped create an early exemplar of 'blow-back' diplomacy: Mugabe was a leader the 'west' would later regret assisting. The rest of this article will concentrate on ZIPA's legacy in the archives and memories of those who helped in its demise.

The British and the Americans had quite different interpretations of ZIPA, reflecting American clarity derived from their tendency to put local variations onto a template dominated by the cold war. In contrast, it appears that few of the British foreign policy and intelligence operatives pigeon-holed ZIPA's radical elements as Soviet pawns. Some saw them as mere tribalists, others perceived democratically inclined socialists, and as often as not the perspectives were mixed. However, both American and British documents reveal that ZIPA was easily confused with ZANU, from which the ZIPA radicals were attempting to extricate themselves. They show too that ZIPA's trust in their Frontline State hosts – especially Mozambique – may have been misplaced. Perhaps most importantly, they illustrate how Robert Mugabe so cleverly said to anyone in power just what they wanted to hear, and how he deliberately and convincingly distorted the reality around him to his benefit. Thus, as western diplomats and observers become aware of the rise of ZIPA in the aftermath of Chitepo's assassination and planned a conference furiously in order to regain the ground towards détente lost after March 1975, one can observe an emerging consensus perception of its radicalism and Mugabe's contrasting ostensible moderation. ZIPA's elimination reflected the convergence of Mugabe's and 'the west's' interests.

ZIPA's archival trail: Britain

On 4 May 1976, five months after ZIPA started its campaign and just as it was hitting Rhodesia's transportation infrastructure, came one of the first recorded indications of British interest. Joan Wicken, Julius Nyerere's 'Political Assistant', met Dennis Grennan in Bonn and told him Nyerere was supporting a 'third force'. Wicken had known Nyerere since 1956 (Jennings 2002; *The Guardian*, 21 December 2004). She also had known the viscerally anti-racist, but almost as passionately anti-Stalinist, dedicated Labour Party activist Grennan since their days at Oxford's Ruskin College in the 1950s, which granted postgraduate diplomas to trade union officials and was visited often by African nationalists. Upon graduation from Southampton University (which he attended after Ruskin), he started up the Ariel Foundation to promulgate anti-racist policy, and then became the Labour Party's and Whitehall's man about Southern Africa. His first posting was as Kenneth Kaunda's adviser after Zambia's independence in 1964. It was there he met Robert Mugabe. Later, when the latter was imprisoned in Rhodesia's capital, Salisbury, Grennan visited him and agreed to look after Sarah (also referred to as Sally) Mugabe, which he did for more than three years, even hosting her in his house (Moore 2005, 2008; interviews with Grennan, 2007, 2008). In the meantime, Wicken had moved to Tanzania to assist Nyerere. She was copied on just about every piece of Whitehall correspondence concerning Tanzania and Zimbabwe. Grennan's record of the Bonn meeting was as follows:

> She said Nyerere was convinced that Smith could only be forced to settle by increased violence. He did not think that even the South Africans would get Smith to negotiate. It was therefore the intention of the 4 presidents [Frontline state Presidents Nyerere, Kaunda, Khama of Botswana and Machel] to get the war under way as quickly as possible. [Thus] ... the 4 presidents had recently agreed that all the freedom fighters would be trained together in one country and as far as possible in the same camp. This should help to get over tribal

> divisions and create a sense of unity on the basis of common objectives, training and experience. ... the training would take place in Mozambique. (National Archives 1976a)

Thus ZIPA entered into Whitehall's record, as the 'one camp' agreed by the Frontline States.

The Bonn meeting was followed by one of Nkomo's many trips to London (Grennan often had to find money within Whitehall for the excessive expenses incurred by Nkomo's trips). Its briefing notes indicate clear awareness of 'troubles in the bush' deriving from the Zimbabwe nationalists' well-known disunity, leaving a vacuum ideal for the arrival of a group such as ZIPA. This message, however, did not see ZIPA in Wickens' benign light:

> The other great risk in failing to achieve a greater measure of unity among the traditional nationalist leaders is that the latter may be supplanted by a new leadership emerging from the ranks of the freedom-fighters with extreme views and an alien ideology. This risk would be diminished if the traditional leaders (or at least Mr Nkomo and Bishop Muzorewa) can form a common front and exercise control over the liberation army. (National Archives 1976b)

As will be seen, the Americans soon discerned 'moderate' inclinations in Mugabe, but the British appeared to be a little slower off the mark in that respect.

On 14 August 1976, Britain's Ambassador to Mozambique, John Lewen, reported back to Whitehall on one of his many meetings with Samora Machel. This meeting was extraordinary because Rhodesia had just begun its horrific raids on Zimbabwean refugee camps, making a clear point to parties sympathetic to Zimbabwe's liberation whilst preparation for the Geneva conference was under way. Lewen's and Machel's discussion about the Zimbabwean struggle made it clear that the terrain in Zimbabwe was not only propitious for the war to be waged without bases in Mozambique (as Lewen had broached), but also offered an alternative interpretation of ZIPA that was quite different from that of 'tribal divisions', as Wicken had argued earlier, or indeed from developing 'extreme views and an alien ideology'. It was that they were plain and simply about political 'leadership'.

> I ... said that looking ahead the most serious obstacle to a settlement was the fragmentation of the nationalist movement. The pressures were building up on the whites to negotiate, but with whom could they or, when it came to transfer of sovereignty, the UK deal? Even ZANU had now split, with a separate Karanga movement [referring to ZIPA]. Machel agreed. There were old quarrels not yet healed. He instanced the murder of Chitepo. But the presidents were still working on the foundation of a united political leadership and thought they would eventaully [sic] succeed. (National Archives 1976c)

At times the British observers saw ZIPA in ethnic terms. Thus it was often seen, as above, as the vanguard of the 'Karanga', a subgroup of the Shona thought to be militarist by nature, and often perceived to be behind Chitepo's earlier assassination, who was ethnically Manyika (see also Sithole 1979). Other observers saw the 'freedom fighters' as possessing an assuredly political identity of their own. For example, when the Minister of State for the Commonwealth, Ted Rowlands, visited Machel after the Lewen conversation, the discussion went like this:

President Machel warned against ignoring the freedom fighters. Any majority government would have to be acceptable to the broad spectrum of guerrillas. If not, a second Vietnam could arise. It was essential that the west backed no group in Zimbabwe in opposition to the freedom fighters. Mr. Rowlands agreed that an interim government would have to represent the broad spectrum of the nationalist movement. There would be no advantage to Britain in legalising a puppet government. (National Archives 1976d)

A few days later, on September 4, the British Rhodesia team sat down with Kissinger in Whitehall (National Archives 1976e). The Atlantic alliance diplomats were effusive in Machel's praise: he was 'the most impressive of the Presidents [showing] the most detailed grasp of the problems posed by the transition period' and was 'unexpectedly pragmatic and unideological' (the 'un' was inserted in handwriting above the typed 'ideological', indicating the recording secretary's Freudian-style slips!). In contrast to the other presidents' 'confused and differing ideas about how to achieve a negotiated settlement … [Machel] knew what he was doing'. That knowledge had much to do with the freedom fighters (conflated by Grennan with the 'Karanga'). They 'would oppose settlement' ('would oppose' being handwritten in the left margin of the document) not based on the 'unconditional surrender' of whites in Zimbabwe. The Whitehall group thought Machel was banking on 'a Frelimo-style regime installed in Salisbury through negotiation because "his men" would come out on top', thus indicating they saw ZIPA as under Machel's control. He was 'more sympathetic than we had expected and anxious to avoid an internationalisation of the war, believing he could achieve his objectives through negotiation'.

Two days before the Whitehall meeting, Rowlands telegrammed from Lagos, arguing that Machel saw

> a more dominant position for [ZIPA] than do the other two [the two being Vorster, and Kissinger, who Rowlands accused of 'selling a different bill' to Vorster and the frontline presidents], and presumably expected that the Mozambique-based Karanga, under Frelimo guidance, will rapidly come to the top in a new Zimbabwe.

The British and Americans agreed with this interpretation of Machel's plans, repeated their unanimous admiration for him, but noted that 'he was deeply suspicious that it was our intention to promote the emergence of a government sympathetic to the West' (Dr Kissinger commented: 'He is right').

Three weeks later, Rowlands reported back from a Botswana meeting with ZAPU leader Joshua Nkomo. He repeated Nkomo's assertion that 'Mugabe was quote controlled by the young men unquote in Mozambique', stalling unity among the politicians (National Archives 1976e).[4] Nkomo suggested that *if* Mugabe agreed to join Nkomo (in what would later be the PF – a *political* diplomatic front representing two *different* armies, reversing ZIPA's attempts at unity from the soldiers up) 'we might take it that [Mugabe] had the backing of the young men (i.e. the freedom fighters)' (National Archives 1976f). These young men, Lewen warned in a later interpretation that saw ZIPA as radical rather than tribal, might 'turn out to be African Palestinians', that is, radical militants liable to fit into the category of 'terrorist' (National Archives 1976g).

In interviews, Dennis Grennan (in his mid-eighties) cannot remember the ZIPA episode, although he recalled Nkomo vividly (disparaged because of his profligate spending and interest in business deals and women before politics), Nyerere (who would appear to be very altruistic but in reality would always be serving his own agenda), Kaunda (who Grennan had to teach to be less trusting and naive, and whose often violent disagreements with Nyerere Grennan had to moderate), Machel (a pragmatist), and Kissinger (whom he advised on his Southern African tours and held in very high esteem). He especially recalled Mugabe: 'very intelligent, but not as intelligent as he thought he was', who had 'no ideology: rather, his ideology was pragmatism' and who treated his wife Sally (admired greatly by Grennan, who praised her for being the Zimbabwe's liberation movement's best London diplomat) 'like a dog: he did not beat her, but just treated her like a nuisance' (Interviews September 2007; June 2008). It seems, though, that he and many of his colleagues viewed ZIPA as an amalgam of ideological and tribal identities, repeating the popular 'anthropological' wisdom that saw the Karanga ethnic group as 'good warriors'. This blend made it easy to assume that Josiah Tongogara and the others in Lusaka's prisons, who were released and their murder charges dropped just as the Geneva conference was beginning, were much closer to ZIPA than was in fact the case. To be sure, ZANU/ZANLA's Tongogara and Hamadziripi and ZIPA's Machingura shared ethnic roots, but this by no means meant they were political allies. Indeed, one of ZIPA's *raison d'êtres* was to go beyond tribalism and nationalism.

It appeared, then, that the British did not quite know what to make of ZIPA. It is not clear if they understood the impact of the group's efforts to forge unity among the liberation forces, or whether they saw ZIPA as 'tribalist' or the importers of 'alien ideologies'. If they were relying on South African intelligence, they may have drawn a blank; according to one officer in those intelligence ranks, ZIPA did not register on their screens.

ZIPA's archival trail: the United States steps in

Well before the British and Americans were discussing Zimbabwe's fate in London, Stephen Solarz, a freshly elected American congressman who later headed Congress's subcommittee on African affairs, paid a visit to Robert Mugabe at the Quelimane house where Frelimo detained him after his arrest. After the 7 July 1976 meeting, Solarz decided Mugabe was the man for the times. According to Solarz, Mugabe scorned Mozambique's economic and political policies, saying: 'Mozambique is a military state and we do not want military rule. We want a civiial [sic] government, democratically elected, and similar to what Tanzania has today' and that an independent Zimbabwe under ZANU control would be governed more like Tanzania and Zambia than Mozambique. He denounced Machel's idea that Zimbabwe's guerrilla conflict should take the form of a 'protracted struggel' [sic], explaining that the 'third force High Command was composed entirely of ZANU military leaders who were loyal to him' and was 'controlled by himself and ZANU Central Committee'. He also dismissed the idea that ZANU and the 'third force' would ever invite foreign troops (implying the Soviet Union or its allies) to assist in liberating Zimbabwe, and said that the UK no longer had a meaningful role to play in resolving the Rhodesian problem (perhaps to stroke the young congressman's patriotic pride). He said unity, including the military unity behind the idea of the 'third force', had been imposed 'on threat of extinction' by Kenneth Kaunda for the détente attempts in late 1974. There were no more ZIPRA (ZAPU) soldiers, they had 'turned out to be completely worthless', refusing to fight 'while their chief, Nkomo, continued to negotiate with Smith. Most of them eventually left the camps'. Mugabe denied that the ZIPRA soldiers 'were being chased away, although he acknowledged that there was friction between the ZANU and ZAPU cadres in the camps'. He told Solarz that there were 20,000 'youngsters over seventeen' trained or under military instruction.

Solarz's report concluded that Mugabe was 'an impressive, articulate and extremely confident individual' with a 'philosophical approach to problems and … well reasoned arguments' reminiscent of Julius Nyerere, 'a man Mugabe obviously admires and respects'. Solarz's next comments indicated that the 'third force' was clearly of concern to those who paid for his journey, and that it was important to ascertain its leadership.

> Whether Mugabe is or is not the leader of the third force, he is … staying close to the fighters and building his bridges for the future. There is no question that he will have to be reckoned with in Zimbabwe's post-independence sweepstakes. (National Security Archives 1976)

Solarz's next stop was 'Saliburg' [*sic* – referring to Rhodesia's capital Salisbury], where he said he might meet Rhodesia's Prime Minister Ian Smith. He asked Mugabe for suggestions of what to do at the meeting. Mugabe said Solarz might consider shooting Smith. No record of such a meeting has been traced.[5]

A few months later, just as the Geneva conference was beginning, the American ambassador in Lusaka sent a telegram to the Secretary of State, the American mission in Geneva, and various African stations (United States of America 1976). Entitled 'Basis for African Unrealism in Geneva', it argued that the militant freedom fighters had been given far too much credit for bringing Smith to the table in Geneva. Therefore, the nationalists' and the Frontline presidents' demands were far-fetched. 'Recent intelligence has reported more of the attitudes of the extreme elements in ZANU and ZIPA than those of ZAPU and Muzorewa's ANC'. Although 'time might modify' the views of 'the ZANLA/ZIPA groups, as well as the recent ZANU prisoners (Tongongara [*sic*]) [who] may be suffering from their isolation … their assessment is an unrealistic one'. The diplomat opined that this view 'greatly exaggerates the effectiveness of the freedom fighters at this stage'.

> If one were to classify Nkomo, Mugabe, and Muzorewa as more realistic and reasonable political leaders, one would at the same time have to recognize that all three are weakened by more radical elements within and outside of their organizations. Mugabe himself is supposed to be more reasonable in private than in public. However his position in ZANU vis a vis Tongongara [*sic*] and the ZIPA freedom fighters is not strong. The latter may be naïve and unrealistic but Mugabe must look to them for support. Similarly, Nkomo, Muzorewa and Sithole need to be careful not to be outflanked by ZANU militancy. (United States of America 1976)

The ambassador may have underplayed ZIPA's contribution to setting the stage for renewed negotiations, and erred in seeing ZIPA and Tongogara as united, but the analysis of Mugabe's weakness regarding the 'freedom fighters' may have been closer to the mark than Solarz's. Combined with Kissinger's heavy warnings to his British ally about the Soviet threat, this sort of analysis mixed into a potent brew.

Kissinger's private letter on 21 October 1976 to Anthony Crosland (which Kissinger suggested Crosland destroy) revealed the *vashandi*'s real stakes. Kissinger chastised Crosland for raising militant African nationalists' hopes. Britain's 'attitude' could encourage 'radical Africans' to 'put forward more and more demands', leading to Russian meddling and 'chaos … and the whole enterprise after all only makes sense as a firebreak to African radicalism and Soviet intervention' (Crosland Papers 1976).

Often, as American foreign policy unfolds, unrealistic and radical political actors are removed from the scene. This is exactly what was prescribed in Washington on 28 January 1977, just when Saul's article on ZIPA appeared in *Southern Africa* and merely a week after Mugabe and Machel packed ZIPA's ideological radicals into Mozambique's prisons. A *Special National Intelligence Estimate* (SNIE, United States of America Central Intelligence Agency 1977), the American intelligence services' 'most authoritative written judgment on national security issues ... [produced] after consulting with all intelligence community members through an interagency process' and distributed to 'key policymakers in both the executive and legislative branches' summarised Rhodesia's prospects after the Geneva conference (Rosenbach and Peritz 2009).[6] It advised dental work for the nationalist movement, suggesting the dangerous ZIPA fang be removed.

Special National Intelligence Estimate: Rhodesia proved to be the post-mortem for both the Geneva conference and *vashandi*. It asserted the commonality of interests between Tongogara and ZIPA (named as such, but as part of 'Robert Mugabe's delegation representing ZANU and ZIPA', in turn a component of the 'new factor' of the PF, a 'loose alliance ... formed for negotiating purposes' that 'enhanced the stature of its leaders by holding the limelight throughout the long negotiations'). The document was a chronicle of ZIPA's death foretold. 'There is', the analysis reads:

> considerable uncertainty surrounding the political role that the guerrillas would play in a post-settlement situation, although it would be an important one. ZIPA leaders presumably would have to have a share of political power in the post-settlement arrangements, in addition to their security role. The guerrilla military forces potentially could wield considerable – even dominant – political power by the threat or use of their arms. Whether this potential would be realized would depend on a number of factors – such as the attractions of rival ethnic leaders, whether the guerrillas could remain unified, what arrangements would be made in the settlement agreement regarding the guerrillas' role. (SNIE, United States of America Central Intelligence Agency 1977, 8)

The report states that Soviet and Cuban ties 'to Nkomo are not as close as they once were' and are 'only beginning to take shape' with Mugabe.[7] The final words on ZIPA are ominous. The Americans were worried that a wide franchise would lead to more voters 'susceptible ... to simplistic and inflammatory rhetoric, a factor which moderates of both races regard as giving a dangerous advantage to the guerrilla-dominated ZANU/ZIPA'. This idea (of posing the Communist threat to moderates as well as Smith's cadre) could 'serve to overcome ... the ingrained revulsion within the white community against striking a deal with the less militant nationalists' (SNIE, United States of America Central Intelligence Agency 1977, 9). It seemed that the USA had decided to back Nkomo because he might be amenable to such notions too, 'but the prospects for Nkomo's leadership and a relatively moderate Zimbabwe government are inversely proportional to ZIPA's strength' (15).

> We believe that the front-line states would agree to restrain and disarm many of the guerrillas, thus diminishing their leaders' own hard line regarding, and claim to power in, the interim government. Conversely, Mugabe would not necessarily have a better chance at assuming the leadership if ZIPA were not defanged: the guerrilla high command would probably put forward its own candidates. In that case, internecine struggles between guerrilla factions would likely ensue. (SNIE 1977, 15)

The radical elements of ZIPA had been defanged indeed, and Mugabe 'had a better chance at assuming the leadership', but what became Mugabe's army certainly was not 'disarmed'.

The aftermath

It may or may not have been coincidental that ZIPA's radical *vashandi* elements already had been 'defanged' (albeit without Tongogara, who possibly surprised the Americans by co-operating with Mugabe and Machel in the operation). The reasons may have been to reduce 'internecine struggles', the number of Soviet Union friends in the region, or to stem the tide of social revolution. Perhaps Britain's interest-free loans of £15 million to Machel helped the process of easing the sharpness of ZIPA's bite (National Archives 1976h, 1976i, 1976j; Moore 2005). Former ZIPA members speculated in 1986 interviews that a large shipment of grain from the USA to Mozambique may have helped. It is unclear to date if Mugabe was acting in concert with Kissinger.[8]

Certainly, for the first half of 1977, official documentation indicates little knowledge of ZIPA's incarceration and indeed Mugabe continued to claim ZIPA as his own and still to be fighting. However, the British embassy official in Maputo doing most of Lewen's work (after the latter's heart attack) sent a note to Whitehall about a chat with his neighbour, a journalist for the Chinese state media (National Archives 1977a). He said the reporter had

> talked about splits with ZIPA, claiming that 'up to 200' of the most radical freedom fighters within ZIPA (including figures like Machingura) had been arrested by the Mozambicans at Mugabe's request last month. I told him that this was the first I had heard of it (and I think it is very unlikely), though it was plain there were tensions within the ZIPA command.

De Chassiron also reported on a BBC journalist's predictions that by the end of 1977, what he called 'ZIPA' would be split, with Tongogara eliminating Mugabe. By mid-year Nyerere was calling for ZIPA's 'revival', as was Mugabe, saying the nationalist movement needed 'organic unity' rather than a 'mechanical merger ... to formulate a joint command structure and training, and to evolve common political and military programmes' (National Archives 1977b). Mugabe announced a new ZANU Central Committee almost simultaneously and said the ZANU axe would fall on the necks of anyone who opposed the 'harmony that binds us all'. A year later he would send yet more 'Karanga' ZANU members to the Mozambican prisons. On 13 August 1979, Rugare Gumbo, one of the members of this ousted group, sent an emissary to the British High Commission in Lusaka with a document detailing the ZIPA story along with his account of what has since been mislabelled the 'Hamadziripi-Gumbo Coup'. The officer who received the document wrote to his superior in London that

> the aim of his visit was to petition HMG [Britain] to make representations to the Mozambican government and to Robert Mugabe to obtain the release of the ZIPA leaders arrested in 1977 and the Hamadziripi/Gumbo group arrested in 1978 ... before the Constitutional Conference, he believing that their influence would be valuable; I really rather doubt whether that would be so. ... I imagine you will not see fit to take any formal action on his 'petition'. (National Archives 1979)

Both groups were released *after* the conference.

The elimination of ZIPA was Robert Mugabe's first exercise of using force to get rid of perceived opposition (there is no evidence that Mugabe had anything to do with Chitepo's assassination, and of course the execution of the Nhari rebels indicates Tongogara's authoritarianism), and thus a beginning of Zimbabwe's democratic deficit. Zimbabwe's future would unfold to see many more axes on many more heads, from *Gukurahundi* (Phimister 2008; Eppel 2004) through to *Operation Murambatsvina* in 2005 (Vambe 2008) and *Mavhoterapapi* (How did you vote?) in 2008 after ZANU-PF's first official election loss. Also, many heads would roll when diamonds were discovered and the military decided to rid the fields of independent miners (Saunders 2014).

Conclusion

This article has contributed a new dimension to our understanding of the relationship between Zimbabwe's liberation struggle and the country's democratic deficit. Most such analyses suffer from an inevitability thesis, which proclaims that the path to dictatorship was inherent from the moment the road to majority rule deviated from liberal constitutionalism (Bratton and Masunungure 2008; Ndlovu-Gatsheni 2008; cf. Moore 2009). Close study of the specific ways in which Robert Mugabe eliminated ZIPA's radicals whilst appropriating their discourse indicates, instead, that Zimbabwe's eventual authoritarianism was not predetermined (Moore and Raftopoulos 2012). In the 1970s, as well as 30 years later, the 'struggles for position' within the state-led processes of Zimbabwe's class formation and primary accumulation were conditioned by complex global, generational and ideological layers (Cramer 2006; Moore 2004). The fact that Mugabe appears to have been supported by 'the west' in this endeavour may help explain his outrage at his former allies spurning him many years later, when they shifted their support to a party more conducive to liberal democracy. At a deeper level, however, the entire affair suggests that over the long term, no assistance to such political actors is better assistance.

Notes

1. Until 1976 the Zimbabwe African National Union's acronym was 'ZANU'. That year, it and the ZAPU formed a united front – the Patriotic Front – for negotiating purposes. In spite of various splits and forced unities since then, the name 'ZANU-PF' remains.
2. The geopolitical territory now called Zimbabwe was called 'Southern Rhodesia' and later 'Rhodesia' during the colonial and minority rule period. 'Zimbabwe' was the name used by the liberation movements. This article will use 'Rhodesia' when discussing the state against which the African nationalists were fighting.
3. The original Mgagao Declaration was written by military officers at the ZANLA training Camp, Tanzania, October 1975.
4. Nkomo was misleading Rowlands. ZIPA was in fact arguing that the Zimbabwean politicians should attend Geneva as a single group to stymie Smith's efforts to divide and rule, and they did not want to be seen to be with Mugabe alone (Mhanda Interview, August 2004).
5. In early 2010 the author attempted, unsuccessfully, to contact Solarz. Solarz died in November 2010. Further archival evidence indicates Henry Kissinger (1977) did not share Solarz's impressions of Mugabe: in the handover routine in January 1977 as Cy Vance took over as Secretary of State for the Jimmy Carter regime, Kissinger opined that Mugabe was

out of control. … absolutely untrustworthy. … If I could have picked someone from the beginning, it would have been Nkomo. … Nkomo is the best. What I don't understand is, is he just a figurehead for Mugabe or does he have power of his own?

Kissinger did state, however, that Mugabe had 'some control' over the guerrillas, thus again indicating that Mugabe had convinced key diplomats of his status vis-à-vis ZIPA.

6. Frank Wisner Jr. asserted that NIEs merely

provide the background to a policy issue that is under debate. They give the scenery, like a play. They're not policy documents: they bring together all of the intelligence available to the United States from various intelligence agencies … because they [address an issue] does not mean that was on the agenda of issues to be addressed by policy makers. (Author interview, 19 November 2013, Washington DC)

From mid-1976 through to the early months of the Carter administration, Wisner was responsible for the State Department's office of Southern African affairs in the Bureau of African Affairs and sent by Kissinger to the Geneva conference to 'shadow and support the British effort'.

7. In interviews ZIPA-*vashandi* leaders confirm approaching the Soviet embassy in Maputo with their plans for unity, and receiving an enthusiastic response. American and/or British intelligence may well have picked this up.

8. Wisner (interview, November 19, 2013) put it thus: 'I can tell you no policy maker in Washington was thinking about the interstices of the Zimbabwean rebel military forces: this was not on anybody's screen'.

References

77 cadres of the African National Council (Zimbabwe), Morogoro Camp. 1976. Memorandum to the OAU Liberation Committee (and the Governments of the Frontline States) (24 August) and Draft Statement on ANC(Z) Massacres (For Publication?) (July). Courtesy of the late Enos Malandu, Harare, 1986.

Astrow, André. 1983. *Zimbabwe: A Revolution That Lost Its Way?* London: Zed Press.

Baumhögger, Goswin, ed. 1984. *The Struggle for Independence. Documents on the Recent Development of Zimbabwe (1975–1980)*, Vol. I. Hamburg: Institute of African Studies.

Bhebe, Ngwabi. 2004. *Simon Vengayi Muzenda: The Struggle for and Liberation of Zimbabwe.* Gweru: Mambo Press.

Booysen, Susan. 2009. "The Presidential and Parliamentary Elections in Zimbabwe, March and June 2008". *Electoral Studies* 28 (1): 150–154. doi:10.1016/j.electstud.2008.09.004.

Bratton, Michael, and Eldred Masunungure. 2008. "Zimbabwe's Long Agony". *Journal of Democracy* 19 (4): 41–55. doi:10.1353/jod.0.0024.

Catholic Commission for Justice and Peace and the Legal Resources Foundation [1997]. 2008. *Gukurahundi in Zimbabwe: A Report on the Disturbances in Matabeleland and the Midlands, 1980–1988.* New York: Columbia University Press.

Chung, Fay. 2006. *Reliving the Second Chimurenga: Memories of the Liberation Struggle*. Uppsala and Harare: Nordic Africa Institute and Weaver Press.

Cramer, Christopher. 2006. *Civil War Is Not a Stupid Thing: Understanding Violence in Developing Countries*. London: Hurst.

Crosland Papers. 1976. London School of Economics and Political Science Special Collections. CC HK>AC 21/10/76.

EISA [Electoral Institute of Southern Africa, written by S. Booysen]. 2008. *EISA Election Observer Mission Report: The Zimbabwe Harmonised Elections of 29 March 2008 Presidential, Parliamentary and Local Government Elections, with Postscript on the Presidential Run-off of 27 June 2008 and the Multi-party Agreement of 15 September 2008*. Johannesburg: EISA.

Eppel, Shari. 2004. "'Gukurahundi': The Need for Truth and Reparation". In *Zimbabwe: Injustice and Political Reconciliation*, edited by Brian Raftopoulos and Tyrone Savage. Cape Town: Institute for Justice and Reconciliation.

Jennings, Michael. 2002. "'Almost an Oxfam in Itself': Oxfam, Ujamaa and Development in Tanzania". *African Affairs* 101 (405): 509–530. doi:10.1093/afraf/101.405.509.

Kissinger, Henry. (2011 [1977]). "Memorandum of Conversation, with Secretary-designate Vance and others, January 19". In *Foreign Relations of the United States 1969–1976 Vol. XXVIII, Southern Africa*, edited by Myra Burton and Edward Keefer. Washington, DC: United States Government Printing Office.

Leys, Colin, and John S. Saul, eds. 1995. *Namibia's Liberation Struggle: The Two-edged Sword*. London: James Currey.

Mandaza, Ibbo. 1986. "Introduction." In *The Political Economy of Transition in Zimbabwe: 1980–1986*, edited by Ibbo Mandaza. Dakar: Codresia.

Martin, David, and Phyllis Johnson. 1980. *Zimbabwe: The Chimurenga War*. London: Faber and Faber.

Mhanda, Wilfred. 2011. *Dzino: Memories of a Freedom Fighter*. Harare: Weaver Press.

Moore, David. 1990. "The Contradictory Construction of Hegemony in Zimbabwe". PhD diss., York University.

Moore, David. 1991. "The Ideological Formation of the Zimbabwean Ruling Class". *Journal of Southern African Studies* 17 (3): 472–495. doi:10.1080/03057079108708288.

Moore, David. 1995. "Democracy, Violence, and Identity in the Zimbabwean War of National Liberation: Reflections from the Realms of Dissent". *Canadian Journal of African Studies/Revue Canadienne des Études Africaines* 29 (3): 375–402. doi:10.2307/486015.

Moore, David. 2004. "The Second Age of the Third World: From Primitive Accumulation to Public Goods?" *Third World Quarterly* 25 (1): 87–109. doi:10.1080/0143659042000185354.

Moore, David. 2005. "ZANU-PF and the Ghosts of Foreign Funding". *Review of African Political Economy* 32 (103): 156–162.

Moore, David. 2008. "Contesting Civil Societies in Zimbabwe's Interregna." Unpublished paper. Durban: Centre for Civil Society, University of KwaZulu-Natal. http://ccs.ukzn.ac.za/files/moorezim100.pdf.

Moore, David. 2009. "Liberation Movements and Democracy in Africa: Beyond the Easy Answers." *Open Space* 2 (5): 56–61.

Moore, David. 2014a. "Death or Dearth of Democracy in Zimbabwe?". *Africa Spectrum* 49 (1): 101–114.

Moore, David. 2014b. "Zimbabwe's Democracy in the Wake of the 2013 Election: Contemporary and Historical Perspectives". *Strategic Review for Southern Africa* 36 (1): 47–71.

Moore, David, and Brian Raftopoulos. 2012. "A Decade of Diminishing Democracy: Zimbabwe 1999–2009". In *Crisis! What Crisis? Exploring the Multiple Elements of Zimbabwe's Crisis*, edited by Sarah Chiumbu and Muchaparara Musemwa. Cape Town: HSRC Press.

Mugabe, Robert. 1977. "Comrade Mugabe Lays the Line at Historic Chimoio Central Committee Meeting". *Zimbabwe News* 13: 5–6.

Mugabe, Robert. 1985. *Zimbabwe African National Union Central Committee Report. Zimbabwe News*, sp. ed. ZANU (PF) Second Congress, August 8–13, 1984, 16(1): 4–32.

National Archives. 1976a. Note for the Record. Prem 16/1092. London. May 6.

National Archives. 1976b. Visit to London of Mr. Joshua Nkomo. Brief No. 1. Prem 16/1092. London. May 18–20.

National Archives. 1976c. To Immediate FCO Telno 156 of 16 August, from John Lewen, Ambassador to Mozambique. CP/020/367/1 FM Maputo 160850Z. London.

National Archives. 1976d. Record of a Meeting between the Minister of State for Foreign and Commonwealth Affairs and the President of Mozambique held in Maputo on 31 August at 10:00 a.m. CP/020/367/1. London.

National Archives. 1976e. Note of a Meeting between Prime Minister and the Secretary of State at 10 Downing Street on September 4 1976. CP/020/367/1. London.

National Archives. 1976f. Minister of State, From Gaborone to Foreign and Commonwealth Office, incl. Pretoria, Washington, Dar es Salaam, Lusaka, UKMIS, Maputo. CP/020/367/1, 29 September 1976, Tel No. 697. London.

National Archives. 1976g. Prem 16/1096, GR 175, Cypher/Cat A FM Maputo, 26 September Your Tel No. 155. London.

National Archives. 1976h. Info Routine Washington and Pretoria, For Secretary of State from Minister of State. Immediate Desk By 021000Z Sep, Cypher Cat A, FM Lagos 0206501 September, Secret, Eclipse, Desk B Y 020002, To Immediate FCO Tel No. 738 of 2.9.76. London.

National Archives. 1976i. Mozambique No. 1. CSQ 093/1(273) 1977. London.

National Archives. 1976j. Mozambique No. 3. CSQ 093/1(139) 1977. London.

National Archives. 1976k. From Lusaka 2308402, Frank Miles, Ambassador to Zambia. CP/011/21 March 1976. London.

National Archives. 1976l. CP/020/367/12 Sept 1976, Maputo 20 August 1976. London.

National Archives. 1977a. China-Mozambique Relations, British Embassy, Maputo, 23 March 1977. CP/020/2. London.

National Archives. 1977b. FCO 36'1926-8. London.

National Archives. 1979. A. J., Hawkes to Miss R. J. Spencer, Rhodesia Department, FCO. CP 011/1, 12 September 1979. London.

National Security Archives. 1976. State Department, Text of Telegram 76Maputo000785 ADP 150 Confidential, CodeL Solarz: Meeting between Congressman Solarz and ZANU leader Edward [sic] Mugabe. NSC-06/020W, declassified 7/19.1990. George Washington University, Washington, DC.

Ndlovu-Gatsheni, Sabelo J. 2008. "Reaping the Bitter Fruits of Stalinist Tendencies in Zimbabwe". *Concerned African Scholars Bulletin* 79 (winter): 21–31.

Ndlovu-Gatsheni, Sabelo J. 2009. *Do 'Zimbabweans' Exist? Trajectories of Nationalism, National Identity Formation and Crisis in a Postcolonial State*. Bern: Peter Lang.

O'Brien, Stephen. 2009. "From Comrade to His Excellency: Mugabe's Rise to Power". *The Australasian Review of African Studies* 30 (1): 26–48.

Onslow, Sue. 2006. "'We Must Gain Time': South Africa, Rhodesia and the Kissinger Initiative of 1976". *South African Historical Journal* 56 (1): 123–153. doi:10.1080/02582470609464968.

Onslow, Sue. 2009. *The Cold War in Southern Africa: White Power, Black Nationalism and External Intervention*. London: Routledge.

Phimister, Ian. 2008. "The Making and Meanings of the Massacres in Matabeleland: Revisiting the Heart of Darkness." *Development Dialogue* 50: 197–214.

Ranger, Terence. 1980. "The Changing of the Old Guard: Robert Mugabe and the Revival of ZANU." *Journal of Southern African Studies* 7 (1): 71–90. doi:10.1080/03057078008708020.

Rosenbach, Eric, and Aki J. Peritz. 2009. *Confrontation or Collaboration? Congress and the Intelligence Community*. Cambridge: Belfer Center, Harvard University.

Saul, John S. 1979. "Transforming the Struggle in Zimbabwe." In *State and Revolution in Eastern Africa*, edited by John S. Saul. New York: Monthly Review Press.

Saul, John S. 2010. *Revolutionary Traveller: Freeze-Frames from a Life*. Winnipeg: Arbeiter Ring.

Saunders, Richard. 2010. "Zimbabwe: Liberation Nationalism, Old and Born Again." *Review of African Political Economy* 38: 123–134.

Saunders, Richard. 2014. "Geologies of Power: Blood Diamonds, Security Politics and Zimbabwe's Troubled Transition." *Journal of Contemporary African Studies*. doi:10.1080/02589001.2014.956501.

Sithole, Masipula. 1979. *Zimbabwe Struggles within the Struggle*. Salisbury: Rujeko.

Smith, David, and Colin Simpson. 1981. *Mugabe*. Salisbury: Pioneer Head.

Tekere, Edgar. 2007. *A Lifetime of Struggle*. Harare: SAPES Books.

Trewhela, Paul. 2009. *Inside Quatro: Uncovering the Exile History of the ANC and SWAPO*. Johannesburg: Jacana.

Tshabangu, Owen. 1979. *The March 11 Movement in ZAPU: Revolution within the Revolution for Zimbabwe*. Heslington: Tiger Papers Publications.

United States of America Central Intelligence Agency. 1977. Special National Intelligence Estimate: Rhodesia, Looking Ahead, Secret, SNIE 72.1-1-77. (Freedom of Information Act). January 28.

United States of America Department of State. 1976. State Message, From Amembassy Lusaka to Sec. State Washington, Geneva to Wisner, 'Basis for African Unrealism in Geneva'. (Freedom of Information Act). October 25.

Vambe, Maurice, ed. 2008. *The Hidden Dimensions of Operation Murambatsvina in Zimbabwe*. Harare and Pretoria: Weaver Press and African Institute of South Africa.

White, Luise. 2003. *The Assassination of Herbert Chitepo: Text and Politics in Zimbabwe*. Bloomington: Indiana University Press.

Liberating development? Rule and liberation in post-independence Tanzania

Leander Schneider

Department of Political Science, Concordia University, Montreal, QC, Canada

Tanzania was a critical ally to the independence movements of Southern Africa, and its post-independence experiences of nation-building became an important model for them. The country was a pioneer in the transformation of liberation movements into governing parties, the formation of the single-party state, the introduction of heterodox socialism *cum* economic nationalism and the rapid emergence of illiberal and authoritarian tendencies in newly liberated countries. This article argues that in Tanzania such authoritarian tendencies were intimately and paradoxically tied up with a principally benevolent commitment to transforming society along egalitarian lines and the rapid advancement of rural development. This commitment bore repressive fruits, however, when it combined with Nyerere's and other politicians' paternalistic view of the peasantry and their belief that they knew best; a framing of postcolonial politics as an ongoing struggle against neo-colonial enemies; and a parallel suspicion that counter-revolutionary, reactionary forces lurked behind a lack of popular enthusiasm for the single-party state's project of establishing Tanzania's particular brand of '*ujamaa*' socialism. The Tanzanian case suggests a complex picture of the nature of authoritarian tendencies in former liberation movements in post-independence Southern Africa; Tanzania's experience shows that there is more, sometimes significantly more, to such tendencies than just the self-serving motives of ruling elites.

'Seek ye first the political kingdom, and all else shall be added unto you', proclaimed Ghana's Kwame Nkrumah. Certainly, Tanzania's post-independence experience would have been far less of a mixed bag for 'liberation' had things been so easy. The country's achievement of political independence from Britain in 1961 was of course a momentous event. Whereas violence accompanied the end of colonialism in many other African countries, in Tanzania the process was peaceful and swift. But as founding President Julius Nyerere often pointed out, political liberation from colonialism merely established an opportunity for, but was no guarantee of, a more *substantial* liberation of Tanzanians. 'Independence asserts our dignity and establishes our opportunity', noted the president. 'The opportunity has now to be used, and our national pride has to be given to the basis of a healthy, educated, and prosperous people' (Tanganyika 1964, vii). Accordingly, on the 10th anniversary of independence, Nyerere identified three stages of the liberation of his country:

The first was that in which we demanded uhuru [freedom/independence] after becoming conscious of the indignity of being ruled by others ... The second stage ... was that of questioning ourselves, defining, and agreeing on the kind of nation we want to build. Now we have agreed that we want to build a nation with true independence, not one which has only 'flag independence'... We shall refuse to allow Tanzania to be a tool or stooge of any nation; but we have also decided that no Tanzanian should be used for the benefit of another Tanzanian. We have agreed that we shall build a nation on the basis of equality, and have rejected the idea of having within our nation a class of masters and a class of servants ... [W]e decided that we would build a nation based on equality and brotherhood – a socialist nation ... Now our Party is entering into its third stage; and this is the stage of actually building and defending that kind of country. (1971, in Nyerere 1973, 333–334)

The struggle for liberation, it was thus clear to Tanzania's political leadership, had not ended with independence; in many ways, the hardest part still lay ahead. Crucially, Tanzania would still have to be liberated from what was often referred to as the 'exploitation of man by man' and the 'unholy trinity of poverty, ignorance, and disease'. '*Ujamaa*' (literally: 'familyhood') socialism and development would bring this fuller liberation for Tanzania.

Nyerere had begun to talk about *ujamaa* around the time of independence – then describing it as an attitude of mind that accepted the equal sharing of prosperity in society (1962, in Nyerere 1966a). By the second half of the 1960s, this general notion had crystallised into a series of proclamations – among them the famous Arusha Declaration of 1967 – and policy proposals announced by Nyerere on behalf of the ruling Tanganyika African National Union (TANU). Those concerning the building of socialism and development in the rural areas would affect the lives of Tanzanians especially significantly. Meant to bring fully meaningful liberation to Tanzania's largely rural, poor population, the country's policies on rural development paradoxically soon turned into coercive campaigns by the state to resettle rural populations into so-called *ujamaa* villages. These were meant to be internally self-governing communities whose establishment would bring scattered rural populations into denser settlements, facilitate the cooperative organisation of economic activities and permit provision of services like health care and water supplies. To the approximately 70% of Tanzanians who were cajoled and coerced – sometimes at gunpoint – to resettle in these villages (a process referred to as 'villagisation'), this 'liberation' of course felt rather like a new tyranny.

This article argues that this turning of an emancipatory vision into an authoritarian reality was inextricably connected to certain discursive framings of Tanzania's situation. A crucial piece in the puzzle of the 'liberational despotism' that took shape in Tanzania was the political elite's conviction that it was justified, and indeed obligated, to force its charges to be free. The following highlights three crucial underpinnings of this conviction. Most prominent was a paternalistic conception of politicians' positioning vis-à-vis 'backward' peasants; ultimately, the peasantry was simply not deemed competent to make decisions regarding how to build a better future for itself – and so politicians had to take charge. Coercion was thus framed to serve a larger goal of liberation. Two other framings likewise worked to legitimise the state's actions while delegitimising alternative voices and resistance. These were a casting of the state's project as a struggle for socialism and its inscription into a pervasive idiom of a continued struggle against colonialism and its remnants. In the struggle against colonial and class enemies, one was either with the ruling party or an enemy of the people. Dissent and resistance, therefore, were the result either of ignorance on the part of backward peasants or of sinister motives. Rather than being recognised as signs that the struggle for liberation was undermining its own goals, dissent and resistance therefore demanded that this struggle be sharpened. While these schemas were of course very much of a particular time and place, they also find echoes, this article suggests, in some of the other cases of post-liberation politics discussed in this special issue.

Rural development and liberation

Julius Nyerere's vision for the development of the Tanzanian countryside appeared to be based on a conception of development that prefigured much of what Amartya Sen would elaborate on more than a quarter of a century later in thinking about 'development as freedom'. In his 1968 paper 'Freedom and Development', a crucial text in defining how development should be achieved and what rural socialism should look like, Nyerere made the point that effective grassroots control over people's development activities was essential because only under such conditions would the people

> have begun to develop themselves as dignified and confident human beings, in a way which is impossible if they simply take orders from someone else. The fact that the orders of an 'expert' may have led to greater output of a crop if they were fully carried out, does not affect this issue. By debating this matter and then deciding for themselves, the people will be doing real development of themselves (1968a, in Nyerere 1973, 69).

Development thus conceived served a dual role in liberation; it would result in freeing people from the yoke of material poverty, and it would be a process that would simultaneously work through and enlarge the people's capacity to make decisions about their own lives. *Ujamaa* villages would be the sites where this double liberation would take place. Nyerere's paper outlines this vision:

> Ujamaa villages are intended to be socialist organizations created by the people, and governed by those who live and work in them. They cannot be created from outside, nor governed from outside. No one can be forced into an ujamaa village, and no official – at any level – can go and tell the members of an ujamaa village what they should do together, and what they should continue to do as individual farmers. No official of the Government or Party can go to an ujamaa village and tell the members what they must grow. ... For if these things happen – that is, if an outsider gives such instructions and enforces them – then it will no longer be an ujamaa village! An ujamaa village is a voluntary association of people who decide of their own free will to live together and work together for their common good. (1968a, in Nyerere 1973, 67)

Five years later, however, Nyerere struck a very different note when, as Tanzanian newspapers reported, he declared that '[t]he issue of living in Ujamaa villages is now an ORDER of the party' (*Uhuru*, 8 November 1973, quoted in McHenry 1979, 108). This pronouncement sped up and spread across the whole country the state's push to move rural Tanzanians to officially registered village sites, which had already been playing out in several regional settings. The means employed to effect this 'villagisation' ranged from encouragement, to orders, to positive and negative inducements (such as promises of aid and the restriction of famine relief to officially registered villages), to outright coercion and violence against property and people. Illustrating some of the worst excesses, a secret 1974 TANU Party report on villagisation in Pwani Region, for instance, recorded the names of 51 residents of Rufiji District who had been injured in various manners, including by whiplashes; some had to be admitted to hospital in serious condition. The report also listed 215 residents of Rufiji who had had their houses burnt down and property destroyed (CCM Party Archives 1974).

Coercive villagisation only became necessary, of course, because people would not gather into *ujamaa* communities on their own accord. There had been some earlier exceptions to this rule; 17 villages in the south of the country under a grassroots group known as the Ruvuma Development Association (RDA), for instance, had been established on a voluntary basis in the early and mid-1960s (compare Schneider 2014). Indeed, this group had been the inspiration behind Nyerere's vision of *ujamaa*. But the tangible demonstration of a beneficial and attractive way of organising production and life that had fed the growth of this group was absent when the state started leaning on rural populations to follow these villages' model, and few if any of the state-sponsored villages ever managed to replicate the successful experience of the Ruvuma villages. This was in part because they lacked the internal political organisation and expanding local expertise and capacity of the villages of the RDA – in good part because the development of such capacity and organisation was undercut from the get-go by the coercive manner in which many of the state-sponsored villages were thrown together. Coercive implementation simply did not make for a good start for community-based development, which, after all, would have to rely on the people's energetic participation.

People resisted resettlement because its benefits were far from obvious to them; besides, it seemed threatening for reasons ranging from the fear that the state wanted to take people's crops to the loss of fertile lands as a result of relocating. While the state's goal was not the seizure of crops, and the economic success and failure of villagisation was in part a function of its mode of implementation itself and not predetermined, the eventual outcome largely proved the sceptics right. In terms of the rural areas' capacity to generate material wealth, villagisation has generally been assessed to have been a step back, and it certainly did not set in motion the kind of economic dynamism that Nyerere had found so inspiring in the RDA. Villagisation's successes proved at best fleeting, even in the much-touted, but typically unsustainable, provision of services such as schools, water supplies and health facilities, despite the immense resources and efforts expended.

But quite besides these economic failings, that a vision of life in the rural areas that had centred on respecting people's free will and disavowed outside instructions and enforcement would turn into a coercive campaign to villagise rural Tanzania throws up a puzzle. Why did Tanzanian state elites not respect the people's reservations and reluctance regarding the state's plans? Was this not what 'liberation' would have demanded?

Development and authority

A crucial piece in this puzzle is how Tanzanian state elites conceived of their role in their new nation, and in particular how they saw themselves positioned vis-à-vis the peasantry. Although Nyerere stressed in 1968 that true development could only be based on voluntary participation and grassroots-democratic organisation, he also held that outsiders had a crucial role to play in setting development in motion. Only through 'education and leadership' could one 'cause people to undertake their own development' as this would help them 'to understand both their own needs, and the things which they can do to satisfy these needs' (1968a, in Nyerere 1973, 61). Nyerere emphasised this task of enlightening the people for a few years, but the underlying assumption – that the people were in need of such enlightenment – already set the stage for different and more forceful forms of interventions. Because the wisdom of the political leadership's educational message – *ujamaa* villages would solve the country's problems – was never open to question, a refusal to endorse this message could only be a sign of ignorance, laziness, conservatism or indeed 'anti-people' stances. Of course, refusal due to such dispositions and motivations could not be tolerated and had to be broken.

This sentiment began to surface prominently from 1970 when progress towards the leadership's vision for the rural areas was not deemed rapid enough. Nyerere now noted:

> I must agree that it is not easy to change the ideas of peasants … [U]nfortunately it is true that many peasants still think that the way to progress is for every individual to have his own little shamba [field]. But such shambas cannot bring progress. (1970, in Nyerere 1973, 155–156)

Likewise, the *Nationalist* newspaper reported on 22 March 1971 that the president had declared that 'Tanzania is still under-developed and it is the peasants and workers who are to blame if no efforts are made to develop the nation'. Others shared such a reading of the situation: Shinyanga's district development director (at the helm of villagisation in the district in 1974), for instance, noted that 'the greater part of the rural peasantry is unaware' and that 'we must remember that the problems of the rural peasantry have been based fundamentally on their traditional outlook and unwillingness to accept change' (Mwapachu 1979, 122, 117). As Boesen, Storgaard Madsen and Moody (1977, 155) comment, such 'attitudes towards ordinary villagers as ignorant, unskilled, subordinate people to whom it was useless to listen' were very widespread. With regard to villagisation, the implication was that one could not go on preaching forever. As Nyerere would put it in 1974: 'For 12 years we have been arguing, arguing. Now we have to deal with the problem of inertia' ('Interview with Nyerere' 1974).

It was not just in the context of villagisation that this way of configuring political authority's role in the new nation and its position vis-à-vis the peasantry yielded compulsion and coercion. One especially striking area in which very similar dynamics were playing out was the re-institution of much-resented colonial agricultural by-laws and minimum acreage rules that commenced immediately after independence. At the first meeting of the newly constituted Tanga Regional Development Committee on 6 April 1962, for instance, Lawi Sijaona, at the time a parliamentary secretary for the Ministry of Local Government and Administration with a prominent political career ahead of him, stated that:

> Government was quite prepared to use methods stronger than persuasion if persuasion failed. Local Authorities would be expected and even required to pass bye-laws [*sic*] which might be necessary to enforce increased agricultural production and these bye-laws [*sic*] would be enforced by the Local Authorities themselves. (Tanzania National Archives 1962a)

The Handeni area commissioner's report on his development plans to the same committee shows that such exhortations from the top fell on very receptive ears among lower-ranking political officers. 'The main difficulty' of his district, judged the commissioner, 'was the laziness of the people, and there could be no increased production until they were made to see that government was determined to enforce increased cultivation. Very stern measures would have to be adopted by the District Council' (Tanzania National Archives 1962b). As is illustrated by a story reported in the *Standard* newspaper on 3 January 1968, Nyerere himself was not generally averse to such measures, although he sometimes also struck a different note. Appearing at a conference for officials of the Ministry of Local Government and Rural Development, 'looking at the Minister … President Nyerere said: "So Bwana [Mister], let us have some bylaws to check this laziness"' (quoted in Ingle 1970, 81–82).

From 1964 to 1968, the number of districts that passed such agricultural by-laws rose from 7 to 43 (out of a total of 60, some of which were urban centres). During the period from 1964 to 1966 the average penalty was 2 months in prison; it rose to 3.6 months in 1967, 4.2 months in 1968 and 6 months in 1969, to decline again to 2 months by 1976 (McHenry 1979, 83–84). The cumulative effect of such measures was that farmers across the country found themselves subject to numerous regulations that imposed minimum acreages or production of particular crops on them.

Popular reactions indicate deep disappointment with what independence had brought for ordinary Tanzanians; clearly, it had not resulted in liberation. During a 1968 villagisation campaign in Handeni, for instance, a local man stood up in front of a meeting and told the following 'story from the reign of the Germans and the British':

> there came a liar [*mtu mmoja 'muongo'*] by the name of J.K. Nyerere and he told us that we should join TANU [the ruling party] to get Uhuru [Freedom/Independence] so that we should govern ourselves and so that we would buy 'Tembo' beer at the market and so that we should not be paying taxes. (Tanzania National Archives 1968a)

Such outspokenness landed the speaker as well as several other 'troublemakers' in jail (Tanzania National Archives 1968b). But the sentiment was apparently quite widely shared: these arrests ushered in protest meetings and demonstrations that resulted in an additional 150 people from the village of Kwabaya being taken into custody. To the political authorities such protests were not in any way justified; in their eyes, they were aimed at derailing the state's valiant efforts to work for the development of the people through building *ujamaa* villages. The Handeni area commissioner cast the issue in this way:

> It is obvious that a group of people at the villages of Kwabaya, Sindeni, Msente and Kideleko, all of which are close to Chanika town, are a danger to the efforts that are being made by people to build ujamaa villages. One big aim of the group of people of these villages is to go to each village in order to coax the residents into not accepting this policy. This is a danger. (Tanzania National Archives 1968b)

In the context of villagisation and related policies, authoritarian interventions aiming to liberate rural Tanzanians from poverty and underdevelopment were consistently cast as justified and necessary because the peasantry was simply not competent to make decisions about what would deliver it into a better future. It was thus in part political elites' deep sense of developmental mission, coupled with a highly hierarchical and paternalistic way of thinking about competence that turned a liberation agenda into a repressive reality for many Tanzanians.

The struggle for socialism

All of this took shape in a context that was increasingly dominated by the idea that Tanzania was engaged in a struggle to establish a socialist society. This specific context only underscored tendencies to brand resistance to the state's policies illegitimate. The struggle for socialism simultaneously called for control by the state and heightened vigilance against elements who, in the context of this framing, were portrayed not just as resisters, but as selfish counterrevolutionaries who deceived the people. The suspicion that the protesters in Handeni mentioned above were coaxing people into rejecting *ujamaa* illustrates well this pattern of thinking. So does the way the ruling party explained its actions in late 1969, when its Central Committee resolved to shut down the RDA, which had been the model for Nyerere's writings about *ujamaa* in the rural areas, and place its member villages under the direct control of the ruling party.[1] Under the heading 'Correct Guidance', the government-controlled newspaper the *Nationalist* cast the move as follows in a lengthy, 26 September 1969 column:

> Ujamaa is Tanzanian Socialism, based on the principles acknowledged by all Tanzanians, for goals cherished by all Tanzanians. As an ideology it must evolve uniformly throughout the country as a condition of unity and correct development. And it is to the Party that one must look for direction and guidance. ... Now before this analysis and detailing of the path which rural people should follow to socialism [in the Arusha Declaration and Nyerere's paper 'Socialism and Rural Development'], some people had got together and set up communities on socialist lines. Through practice if not definition they were evolving their pockets of socialism in a wilderness still not impelled on to socialist transformation. The Party gave such associations its encouragement. ... But the Party now has defined the idea of socialism and it's preparing the mechanism for implementing it in rural areas. The ujamaa village is a model of socialism in rural areas and the Party and its government has arrangements in hand for the development of these villages politically, socially and economically. There was thus clearly the danger that if matters continued as they were we would have a mushroom[ing] of 'Ujamaa' villages representing at the most extreme, every shade of [the] idea of socialism. Already some regions were talking of starting their own Ujamaa village development associations. ... But they can only prosper if they are TANU communities, inspired by its principles, politically guided by, and looking up to TANU for assistance. The decision by the Party to take charge of all Ujamaa villages was a correct, logical, political and ideological necessity.

Putting aside other reasons that contributed to the move to shut down the association, this public explanation laid out a claim that centralisation, party and government control and uniformity were essential for building socialism. Putting Tanzanian politics into the context of the struggle for socialism thus reinforced a tendency of forcefully asserting the state's authority and dealing with oppositional elements. In the context of villagisation, compulsion was thus justified as 'resisters' were branded 'kulaks'[2] and 'proto-capitalists'. So besides being 'conservative' and 'stubborn', some farmers were also class enemies, 'coaxing' (as the above report on the Handeni protests had it) the majority into a false consciousness about their real interests.

Around the beginning of the 1970s, such labelling was heightened when talk of socialism shifted from an emphasis on facilitating the growth of the socialist project among its (potential) sympathisers in pragmatic ways to a stress on the need to confront the enemy in struggle. Events such as the fatal shooting of Regional Commissioner Klerruu, a driving force behind villagisation, by a farmer on 25 December 1971 fuelled such rhetoric (see the *Daily News*, 14, 15, 19 September and 3 October 1972 on the farmer's trial). The dramatic reshuffle of the ranks of the state apparatus in early 1972 also fed into this sharpening of positions; one of the victims of this 'purge', Abdul Babu, who himself was in fact considered among the more radically leftist politicians in Tanzania, described it thus:

> In our place were appointed some very junior and inexperienced 'technocrats' whose only qualification for such senior appointments was their total and uncritical loyalty to President Nyerere personally. They were all 'yes-men', described by Nyerere as the 'believers', as in religion (*waumini* in Kiswahili). (Doornbos 1996, 330)

Many of these 'believers' may have been more deeply steeped in the rhetoric of class struggle and the need for a vanguard than the old guard. Three snapshots of the University of Dar es Salaam and its shifting positioning in this unfolding political history suggest that such a generational *cum* ideological shift was indeed taking place. In 1966c, Nyerere's suspension of the entire student body had been prompted by student protests against the introduction of two years of National Service, consisting of training and work, after graduation. Contrast this picture of student 'conservatism' and defence of privilege with 1969–1970, when Nyerere was contending with a very different phenomenon: growing left 'radicalism' at the university. Although such radicalism may well have been a minority stance, the barrage of Marxist analyses of the Tanzanian situation emanating from the university was indicative of a broader spirit of the time. Indeed, it was too much even for the self-proclaimed socialist government: after the publication of Issa Shivji's seminal essay 'Tanzania: the Silent Class Struggle', the student magazine *Cheche* ('The Spark' – named after the paper Lenin founded) was shut down in 1970. Likewise, in 1978, a march of 1500 students protesting against wage increases of high-ranking government officials would be broken up by the police (Saul 1973; Coulson 1982, 224–230).

In the political rhetoric and practice of the country, one may thus detect what could be called lower-case 's'ocialism – that had room for flexibility, dispersed authority and players other than the state – being replaced with upper-case 'S'ocialism. This emphasised the societal scale (rarely devoting much intelligent thought or energy to anything below that level); acted through the state as the lead-player; focused on 'class struggle' (rather than the concrete working out and facilitation of socialist life and production); and stressed ideology and revolutionary consciousness-raising over pragmatism. This shift contributed to channelling Tanzania's efforts at building socialism in a centralised and authoritarian direction; tragically, it also undermined these efforts in terms of their aspiration to bring liberation both in the economic and the political sphere. Vanguardism was a key ingredient in the increasingly undemocratic edge of Tanzanian socialism; as John Saul, a participant in this history, has recently wondered: 'Is it a kind of paternalism, or perhaps a certain brand of residual Stalinism, that made it so difficult for many of us on the left to take full account of the import of such [authoritarian] actions?' (2005, 150).

Manichaeanism in post-colonial times

This turn to 'S'ocialism in Tanzania was one important contributor to a certain Manichaeanism in the framing of the practices of Tanzanian politics.[3] How the country's post-colonial situation was discursively negotiated was another. Authoritarian tendencies were rooted in part in how TANU's beginnings as an anti-colonial movement continued to play into a conception of the nationalist/ruling party as the only rightful representative of all Tanzanians. In drawing a contrast between European and African parties, Nyerere made this claim – and its grounding in the party's anti-colonial origins – explicit:

> Our own parties ... were not formed to challenge any ruling group of our own people; they were formed to challenge the foreigners who ruled over us. They were not, therefore, political 'parties' – i.e., factions – but nationalist movements. And from the outset they represented the interests and aspirations of the whole nation. (1963, in Nyerere 1966b, 198)

With independence won, such claims of TANU's national inclusiveness and a Manichaean sense of politics as a struggle in which TANU played the part of defender of the nation continued to underpin the party's sense of itself as the only legitimate political force in the country. A series of internal and external events heightened the perceived need to hold the political reins tightly, lest the worthy cause be lost. Portuguese repression in Mozambique, Ian Smith's regime in Rhodesia, and coups in African nations, often suspected or known to have been executed with 'imperialist' support, demonstrated that the threat was real (Coulson 1982, 142–143, 299–311).

In this political culture and climate, voices both within and outside the party that did not conform to the tightly constrained boundaries of legitimate (i.e., non-dissenting) politics were quickly and decisively silenced. Increasingly, political legitimacy was earned by dutifully toeing TANU's line. Organisationally, this was visible in ethnic associations and other political parties being banned in 1961–1963 (Brennan 2005); the bringing of the independent labour unions into the TANU fold in 1962–1964 (Coulson 1982, 137–140); and the press's placement under the president's direct control and incorporation into the party's organisational network in 1967–1972 (Chachage 1997; Tordoff and Mazrui 1972, 437–440).

The ubiquity of the vocabulary of the '(neo)colonial enemy' in these as well as many 'everyday' political events in the country is an indication of the constitutive role that the framing of Tanzania's situation as *still* (rather than finally) post-colonial played in structuring politics as a deeply Manichaean enterprise. Observe, for instance, the Party leadership's rebuke of the aforementioned 1966 student protesters' claim that 'they could be against TANU, Afro-Shirazi Party [Zanzibar's ruling party], the Government and the President but not against the nation', published in the *Nationalist* on 29 October 1966:

> From the inception of TANU and Afro-Shirazi the people have always rallied and supported the correct line of the leadership of these parties; and it was precisely due to the people's endorsement of the party's policies that opposition parties failed on the mainland before and after independence, this led to the establishment of a one Party State.... The faith of the people in the two parties has stood the test of time and goes much deeper than it can be imagined by our armchair philosophers on the Hill [the university] who have succumbed to be used as tools of neo-colonialism.... We wish to state clearly that we regard as enemy No.1 any person who avertly [*sic*] or covertly tries to divide our ranks.

Irreducible to 'just' instrumentally deployed rhetoric (although it could be that too, of course), such framings contributed to the perverse dynamics of a liberation movement turning into a regime with decidedly oppressive features.

Conclusion

What to make of the quick emergence of illiberal and repressive tendencies in newly liberated Tanzania? This article has argued that political elites' understanding of their society and their own role and position in history is a crucial dimension of this story. Of course, making comparisons between the Tanzanian experience of the 1960s and 1970s and later post-liberation politics in Southern Africa has significant limitations. For one, the sense of developmentalist mission witnessed in Tanzania, coupled with a willingness to go in for a major programme of social and economic engineering, certainly epitomised its particular time, and is, therefore, in crucial respects a thing of the past. One can argue (and some will lament) that with the end of the cold war a 'struggle for socialism' is likewise not likely to top the political agenda again any time soon; indeed, many of the illiberal and repressive dimensions of post-liberation politics in Tanzania's southern neighbours may be attributable to a political agenda that aims not at bringing an egalitarian society to the masses but to amass wealth for the political classes. Fully acknowledging these material drivers as central to the shortcomings of more recent liberations, the casual observer may nonetheless be struck by some remarkable similarities between the Tanzanian past and how Southern African anti-colonial leaders have looked at their rule and the basis of their legitimacy. The gesture back to one's role as a liberator in particular is of course a politically efficacious slogan that is often instrumentally deployed. But, as a glimpse back at the Tanzanian story suggests, it may also be more than that: a whole narrative framing that explains and legitimates the new rulers' claim to a natural right to rule, if not in the eyes of their diminishing following, then at least in their own.

Notes

1. This puzzling move cannot be explained in detail here (see Schneider 2014); suffice it to say it proved very harmful to the associated villages and was a significant episode in a broader history of a forceful assertion of the state's authority.
2. The term kulak originated in Russia and referred to relatively affluent and independent peasant farmers who were viewed as class enemies of the Russian revolution by the Bolsheviks and systematically eliminated as a social category.
3. The term Manichaeanism denotes a worldview that sees the world as rigidly divided into good and evil.

References

Boesen, Jannik, Birgit Storgaard Madsen, and Tony Moody. 1977. *Ujamaa: Socialism From Above.* Uppsala: Scandinavian Institute of African Studies.

Brennan, James R. 2005. "The Short History of Political Opposition and Multi-Party Democracy in Tanganyika, 1958–1964." In *In Search of a Nation: Histories of Authority and Dissidence in Tanzania*, edited by Gregory H. Maddox and James L. Giblin, 250–276. Oxford: James Currey.

CCM Party Archives. 1974. "Taarifa ya Uhamiaji Vijijini Vya Maendeleo Mkoani Pwani 1974. 3/118 [Report on Resettlement in Development Villages in Pwani Region 1974]." Dodoma.

Chachage, Chachage Seithy L. 1997. "Democracy and the Fourth Estate in Tanzania." In *Political Culture and Popular Participation in Tanzania*, edited by Research and Education for Democracy in Tanzania (REDET) Project, 73–85. Dar es Salaam: Research and Education for Democracy in Tanzania (REDET) Project, University of Dar es Salaam.

Coulson, Andrew. 1982. *Tanzania: A Political Economy*. Oxford: Clarendon Press.

Doornbos, Martin R. 1996. "A.M. Babu: 'The Outline'." *Review of African Political Economy* 23 (69): 324–333. doi:10.1080/03056249608704206.

Ingle, Clyde R. 1970. "Compulsion and Rural Development in Tanzania." *Canadian Journal of African Studies* 4 (1): 77–100. doi:10.2307/483743.

Interview with Nyerere: Tanzania July 7, 1974 – Saba Saba Twenty Years After, *African Development, Special Tanzania Supplement*, July 1974.

McHenry, Dean E. 1979. *Tanzania's Ujamaa Villages: The Implementation of a Rural Development Strategy*. Berkeley, CA: Institute of International Studies, University of California.

Mwapachu, Juma Volter. 1979. "Operation Planned Villages in Rural Tanzania: A Revolutionary Strategy for Development." In *African Socialism in Practice: The Tanzanian Experience*, edited by Andrew Coulson, 114–135. Nottingham: Spokesman Books.

Nyerere, Julius K. 1966a [1962]. "Ujamaa – The Basis of African Socialism." In *Freedom and Unity. Uhuru na Umoja: A Selection from Writings and Speeches 1952–1965*, edited by Julius K. Nyerere, 162–171. Oxford: Oxford University Press.

Nyerere, Julius K. 1966b [1963]. "Democracy and the Party System." In *Freedom and Unity. Uhuru na Umoja: A Selection from Writings and Speeches 1952–1965*, edited by J. K. Nyerere, 195–203. Oxford: Oxford University Press.

Nyerere, Julius K. 1966c. *Freedom and Unity. Uhuru na Umoja: A Selection from Writings and Speeches 1952–1965*. Oxford: Oxford University Press.

Nyerere, Julius K. 1968 [1967]. "Socialism and Rural Development." In *Freedom and Socialism. Uhuru na Ujamaa: A Selection from Writings and Speeches 1965–1967*. edited by J. K. Nyerere, 106–144. Dar es Salaam: Oxford University Press.

Nyerere, Julius K. 1973 [1968a]. "Freedom and Development." In *Freedom and Development. Uhuru na Maendeleo. A Selection from Writings and Speeches 1968–1973*. edited by J. K. Nyerere, 58–71. Dar es Salaam: Oxford University Press.

Nyerere, Julius K. 1968b [1967]. *Freedom and Socialism. Uhuru na Ujamaa: A Selection from Writings and Speeches, 1965–1967*. Dar es Salaam: Oxford University Press.

Nyerere, Julius K. 1973 [1970]. "A Survey of Socialist Progress." In *Freedom and Development. Uhuru na Maendeleo. A Selection from Writings and Speeches 1968–1973*, edited by J. K. Nyerere, 150–158. Dar es Salaam: Oxford University Press.

Nyerere, Julius K. 1973 [1971]. "Ten Years after Independence." In *Freedom and Development. Uhuru na Maendeleo. A Selection from Writings and Speeches 1968–1973*, edited by J. K. Nyerere, 262–334. Dar es Salaam: Oxford University Press.

Nyerere, Julius K. 1973. *Freedom and Development. Uhuru na Maendeleo. A Selection from Writings and Speeches 1968–1973*. Dar es Salaam: Oxford University Press.

Saul, John S. 1973. "Radicalism and the Hill." In *Socialism in Tanzania: Volume 2 (Policies)*, edited by Lionel Cliffe and John S. Saul, 289–292. Dar es Salaam: East Africa Publishing House.

Saul, John S. 2005. *The Next Liberation Struggle: Capitalism, Socialism, and Democracy in Southern Africa*. Toronto, ON: Between the Lines.

Schneider, Leander. 2014. *Government of Development: Peasants and Politicians in Postcolonial Tanzania*. Bloomington, IN: Indiana University Press.

Tanganyika. 1964. *Tanganyika Five-Year Plan for Economic and Social Development, 1st July, 1964-30th June, 1969*. Dar es Salaam: Government Printers.

Tanzania National Archives. 1962a. "Minutes of the Regional Development Committee Meeting, April 6, 1962." 513/P4/9/I. Dar es Salaam, Unpublished.

Tanzania National Archives. 1962b. "Minutes of the Regional Development Committee Meeting, December 20, 1962." 513/P4/9/I. Dar es Salaam.

Tanzania National Archives. 1968a. *Mgomo wa Vijiji vya Ujamaa vya 1. Vikomba 2. Kilimilang'ombe* [Sabotage of 1. Vikoma and 2. Kilimilang'ombe Ujamaa Village] by Divisional Executive Officer Chanika, August 2, 1968." 513/D3/14. Dar es Salaam, Unpublished.

Tanzania National Archives. 1968b. "Taarifa Kuhusu Vijiji vya Ujamaa, Handeni, October 13, 1968 [Report Concerning Ujamaa Villages, Handeni, October 13, 1968]." 513/D3/14/II. Dar es Salaam, Unpublished.

Tordoff, William and Ali A. Mazrui. 1972. "The Left and the Super-Left in Tanzania." *Journal of Modern African Studies* 10 (3): 427–445. doi:10.1017/S0022278X00022643.

From liberation movement to party machine? The ANC in South Africa

Roger Southall

Department of Sociology, University of the Witwatersrand, Johannesburg, South Africa

This article contributes to a growing literature on the character of leadership, democracy and governance espoused by post-liberation governments, focusing on the African National Congress (ANC) as a political party. The article provides a brief overview of the two most common approaches to analysing the ANC's transition from a national liberation movement to a political party in an electoral democracy, the *dominant party* approach and what is termed the *Fanonesque* perspective. Neither is found to be wholly satisfactory, for largely the same reason – their tendency to present what is effectively a caricature of the ANC, by selectively highlighting features of its practices that conform to a pre-determined pathology, rather than acknowledging the ANC's complexity, variability and essentially contested nature. In developing an alternative approach, the paper draws from an earlier body of literature on single-party–dominant states in post-independent Africa that was empirically driven and comparative in nature. Such an approach can help us develop a more realistic, less sensationalist interpretation of ANC rule in South Africa.

The suggestion that the ruling African National Congress (ANC) needs to complete a transition from a national liberation movement (NLM) to a democratic political party has been central to discussions about the quality of South Africa's democracy. Often embedded in this discussion is the assumption that NLMs are ideological, centralist and authoritarian, whereas to perform competitively within a liberal democracy, parties need to become pluralistic, participatory and pragmatic. A second perspective suggests, in essence, that the ANC has sloughed off too much of its NLM character and has taken on too much of the character of a modern party; that is, it has abandoned the constraints of a transformative ideology, become too open to external forces and lost its popular class character. The two approaches concerned are that of the *dominant party* and what I shall term a *Fanonesque* perspective. Both provide for powerful analyses, yet they share a common weakness, in that both depict what is essentially a caricature of the ANC, rather than properly capturing its complex and contested nature. To move beyond the weaknesses of these perspectives, there is considerable value in revisiting some of the early literature on political parties in post-colonial Africa, which emphasises the successful adaptation of NLMs to post-colonial settings, including their capacity to manage and incorporate a significant degree of internal diversity and dissent. I will illustrate this value by reference to the character of the ANC under Jacob Zuma.[1]

The dominant party approach

The identification of the ANC as a dominant party starts from its overwhelming electoral majority and apparent invincibility at the polls. Basing themselves on Pempel (1990), Giliomee and Simkins (1999) define dominant parties as those that dominate electorally for a prolonged period, lead in the formation of governments and determine the public agenda. Further, they argue there is a fundamental tension between dominant party rule and democracy. Whereas party dominance can lead to competitive democracy (as in Sweden), it can also lead to sham democracy and authoritarianism (as in Nazi Germany). They argue that in contrast to the Scandinavian precedent, dominant parties in semi-industrialised countries are far more likely to abuse their power, because their control over the state is more fragile and they have difficulty establishing autonomy from capitalist interests.

This leads on to the following assertions about ANC rule: first, elections take on the broad character of a 'racial census,' with the overwhelming Black majority of the electorate regularly pledging their support to the ANC. Accordingly, opposition parties become marginalised. Second, although the 1994 interim constitution established nine provinces under a form of federalism, the ANC has used its control of the hierarchical state machinery it inherited to pursue greater centralisation. Third, whereas both the 1993 and 1996 constitutions insist upon public service neutrality, the ANC has followed the historical example of the previously ruling National Party in subverting the independence of the state machinery, notably through the practice of 'deploying' party loyalists to public positions. This blurring of party and state has undermined the liberal ideal of the separation of powers and marginalised parliament. Fourth, the ANC has tended to delegitimise opposition by asserting a crude majoritarianism that results in the alienation of minorities. Often, this has taken an explicitly racial character, with opponents accused of promoting white interests. Finally, the ANC has adopted the principles of democratic centralism (borrowed, in essence, from the Communist Party of the Soviet Union) and utilised these to curb internal dissent (Giliomee, Myburgh, and Schlemmer 2001). The broad thrust of the dominant party thesis is that the ANC has rendered itself largely unaccountable, and despite its regular return to the polls, constitutes a threat to democracy. Prolonged concentration of power leads to abuse, and only the presence of opposition parties as viable alternative governments will ensure the success of democracy.

Conservative and liberal academics and the Democratic Alliance (DA), the major opposition party, have propounded the dominant party thesis most vigorously. Undoubtedly, it has proved a powerful tool for analysing the ANC in power: for instance, there are strong grounds for arguing that under President Mbeki, the ANC centralised power within both party and state, clawed back ground it had lost during the constitutional negotiations by curbing provincial autonomy and blurred party–state relationships by pursuing its deployment strategy (Southall 2005). Nonetheless, the thesis has lent itself to gross exaggeration, notably in its suggestion that the ANC is quasi-totalitarian in its capacity to exert its authority over state and society.

In contrast, critics of the dominant party thesis have stressed that it was the ANC that was the harbinger of democracy in South Africa and the force primarily responsible for the human rights–based nature of the constitution. They say it continues to secure its electoral dominance because it retains the organisational capacity to mobilise popular support at election time. Thus, whilst a 'weak' notion of the ANC as a dominant party can be useful (Southall 2001), strict application of the thesis tends to run up against the messiness of South African reality. One of the limitations of the dominant party thesis is its assumption of the ANC's quasi-totalitarian character, in the form of 'democratic centralism', which implies the party is controlled by an elite that imposes its views upon those below. Yet, manifestly, this does not describe the ANC today, as was demonstrated by the defeat of Thabo Mbeki when he ran for a third term as president of the ANC at Polokwane in December 2007, and his subsequent ousting from the state presidency in September 2008. There are a variety of interpretations of the meaning of Polokwane (Southall 2009). What is clear is that the Congress of South African Trade Unions (COSATU) and the South African Communist Party (SACP) significantly mobilised the Zuma campaign by securing the triumph of pro-Zuma candidates through the ANC's internal electoral procedures, leading up to the all-important ANC National Conference at Polokwane. That Zuma's victory was far from unanimous (Mbeki won around 40% of the votes), there were significant variations in the support each candidate obtained from different parts of the country, and many structures of the party were themselves divided between the two candidates, all point to the lack of unanimity. So much, we might say, for the salience of democratic centralism! In short, the 'dominant party' thesis may well illuminate dimensions of the ANC's behaviour as a ruling party, but it fails rather miserably to account for changes within it. Nor does it describe what social forces the ANC represents, because it fails to explore any wider relationship between the ANC and other 'dominant' forces within society, notably large-scale capital. Those it leaves to followers of the footsteps of Frantz Fanon.

Fanon in Southern Africa

'The Revolution Betrayed'[2] is, we may reluctantly concede, almost as old as the idea of social revolution itself. Human history displays a litany of frustrated revolutionary hopes, of Utopia postponed. In Southern Africa, where national liberation struggles against white supremacy, colonialism and apartheid were conflated into struggles for socialism, it is scarcely surprising that disillusion abounds, since capitalism reigns supreme today. Nor is it surprising that those disappointed with outcomes of liberation struggles should turn to Fanon for explanation.

The national bourgeoisie that takes power at the end of colonialism, argued Fanon, is an underdeveloped class, small in number, lacking economic power and primarily located in service rather than directly productive occupations. Lacking intellectual resources, it seeks little more than to step into the shoes of the departing colonials, transferring their resources into its own hands through strategies of nationalisation and Africanisation. Once in control of key posts, it will insist that big foreign companies should deal with it directly, whether they simply want to keep their connections with the country or to open it up. Thus, 'the national middle class discovers its historic mission: that of intermediary' (Fanon 1974, 122). Although often prepared to resort to defensive racism against a cynical Western bourgeoisie, the national bourgeoisie nonetheless seeks to emulate the latter's lifestyle and ultimately, to identify with it. It engages in 'scandalous enrichment' and 'immoderate money making' and plunges into 'the mire of corruption and pleasure'

(Fanon 1974, 134–35). In such circumstances, 'the economic channels of the young state sink back inevitably into neo-colonialist lines' (Fanon 1974, 134), dependent on external capital and hand-outs.

Fanon's characterisation of the neo-colonial situation has enjoyed wide application, and it is scarcely surprising that its influence should spread to post-liberation Southern Africa. Let us take, for example, the analysis provided by John Saul (2008) in a bitter essay that takes as its cue the statement offered by George Dangerfield (1997, 148) concerning the fate of the British Liberals following their triumph at the polls at the end of World War I: they emerged from the fray 'flushed with one of the greatest victories of all time, yet from that victory they never recovered'. Something similar, Saul opines, can be said of Mozambican liberation movement Frelimo, Angola's People's Movement for the Liberation of Angola (MPLA), Namibia's South West African People's Organization (SWAPO), Zimbabwe's Zimbabwe African National Union – Patriotic Front (ZANU-PF) and the ANC. Although still in power, none has lived up to their promise of genuine national liberation. The importance of their initial victories (over colonialism, racism and apartheid) should never be minimised, yet the socialist hopes they embodied have been frustrated. In all cases, they have succumbed to political and moral degeneration. In Mozambique, corruption and pursuit of individual profit have undermined the legitimacy of Frelimo party leaders, with the election of Guebeza as president in 2002 – 'holder of an expansive business network' (Saul 2008, 156) – signalling wholehearted commitment to a neo-liberal agenda. The situation is likewise in Namibia, where the party elite lives in luxury, disregarding the abject poverty of the majority, and Zimbabwe, where Mugabe's ZANU-PF has engaged in vicious domestic repression of the MDC, the 'most promising example we have yet seen of a progressive "post-liberation movement"' (Saul 2008, 162–163). Yet South Africa provides the most disappointing of case of 'false decolonisation', for by embracing capitalism, the ANC has 'squandered an opportunity of world historic proportions' (164). Why, asks Saul, has this happened to liberation movements that had promised so much?

Saul refutes the suggestion that leaders of the different NLMs adopted capitalist strategies because they were the only realistic ones available. To be sure, the principal reason he adduces for liberation movements to have followed a capitalist path was that they were pressured by the World Bank, IMF and western governments to join the global capitalist game that such players invented and continue to control. Under such circumstances, regional leaders might view capitalism as the only strategy capable of providing for development. Thus some, perhaps most clearly demonstrated by President Mbeki and his Finance Minister, Trevor Manuel, may have opted for capitalism hoping it would provide sufficient surplus to allow the government to pursue social policies capable of alleviating social inequality and injustice. However, while this latter option might be possible in South Africa, to a limited extent, it is much less plausible in neighbouring countries that are located even more at the periphery of global capitalism. Elsewhere, leaders may have calculated that challenging capitalism and imperialism would prove too costly, destabilising and ultimately futile. In these circumstances, it would scarcely be shocking if they opted for self-enrichment. Thus, Saul provides an explicitly Fanonesque explanation involving the new elites selling-out the revolution, their comfortable adjustment to neo-colonialism, the diversion of revolutionary class consciousness amongst the majority into racial consciousness, and the deep penetration of market values and consumerism into society. Saul's conclusions follow in the footsteps of analysts such as Patrick Bond (1998, 46), also writing on South Africa, and Henning Melber (2007) with regard to Namibia.

Aspects of the analysis can be illuminating, importantly locating the one-time liberationist bourgeoisie within a context of global capitalism, imperialism and dependence. However, ultimately the Fanonesque perspective presented by Saul and others tends to substitute 'class' for 'party', that is, that there seems to be an assumption that, even allowing for internal squabbles about the allocation of rewards and a few ersatz debates about policy alternatives, the liberation movements have become nothing more than instruments of political domination and crude economic accumulation for the post-colonial bourgeoisie. Now, this may describe what has happened in Angola, Mozam-bique, Namibia and Zimbabwe (although this roll call contains quite different experiences), but is it not too simple to apply the formula to the ANC?

The uniformity of analysis provided by the Fanonesque perspective reflects Fanon's own one-dimensional position on the party. The political party in the underdeveloped country, he writes, claims to be the embodiment of the entire nation yet becomes a dictatorship, charging itself with the task of controlling the masses and clamping down on dissent. It may also deal with discontent by discovering 'the need for a popular leader to whom will fall the dual role of stabilising the regime and of perpetuating the domination of the bourgeoisie', a description which many might feel beautifully describes Zuma (Fanon 1974, 133). For party militants, the party represents a short-cut to private ends, a post in government and the prospect of a career. Yet as with the theory of party dominance, the Fanonist perspective ultimately fails to provide an explanation for internal party contestation and change. Fanonists place their faith in radical social movements, which will reinstate the struggle against global capitalism in alliance with national and international partners, a kind of mirror image to the faith in opposition parties expressed in the dominant party thesis. In both cases, the scenarios offered are depressingly long term. Is there a mode of explanation that might better reflect the present reality of the ANC – its manifest ability to win elections and conduct internal debates, its deep divisions and its openness to democracy from below? Is there a mode of analysis that takes the ANC as a *political party* seriously?

African precursors

Let us turn our attention away from South Africa to the classic study of the trajectories of the victorious nationalist parties in Ghana, Senegal, Mali and Ivory Coast conducted by Aristide Zolberg (1966) entitled *Creating Political Order: The Party States of West Africa*. While countering the dominant party thesis, the book also debated the ghost of Fanon, becoming intellectually trapped by neither. All four states Zolberg examined saw the emergence of dominant parties after the handover of power to nationalists. Zolberg's analysis proceeds as follows. Nationalist parties triumphed following an initial spurt of mobilisation that combined the spirit of post–World War II popular aspiration with effective communication, organisation and courage, despite lacking significant financial means. These parties won pre-independence elections, but the degree of popular support they received was limited because electoral registration rates were quite low and minority parties often took a substantial slice of the vote.

After assuming office, nationalist parties benefited by gaining access to well-paid jobs, state resources and control over national budgets, which allowed them to determine who would obtain benefits and where they would be located. Thereafter, electorates were enlarged, while at the same time, the authority of parliaments and African executives increased. Nationalist parties, in short, benefited because numerous individuals and groupings identified with them as perceived winners; yet, they risked fragmentation when new political entrepreneurs entered the game, competing for control of the new institutions. Very often, political entrepreneurship entailed an appeal to loyalties such as ethnic affinities. This, in turn, threatened to render a nationalist movement nothing more than another ethnic or regional organisation. In response, the nationalist parties stepped up their organisation (through extension of party branches and so forth) and increased control from the centre, perhaps accompanied by ideological radicalisation. Because their organi-sational capacity was superior to that of their rivals, they were able to consolidate their electoral and political dominance, in some cases obviating the danger of displacement by installing themselves as single parties with a revolutionary ideology. The latter proclaimed the necessity of national unity under the aegis of the party, as most famously declared by then-President Nkrumah: 'The CPP is Ghana and Ghana is the CPP'. 'National unity', then, was obtained by suppressing the opposition and electoral manipulation.

The reality behind the emergence of so-called 'revolutionary mobilising' regimes proved very different from the communist model they sought to emulate. Although such parties aspired to mobilise the entire nation, their capacity to do so rarely extended beyond periodic electioneering. Participant members were relatively few, and support had both regional and ethnic dimensions. 'They had a large head in the capital but fairly rudimentary limbs', although they spoke the language of democratic centralism, internal structures of communication, accountability and control only functioned intermittently. Indeed, David Apter, one of the earliest observers of the Convention People's Party in Ghana, referred to it as 'a Tammany type machine with a nationalist ideology' (Zolberg 1966, 22).[3]

Single-partyism led to the 'party state', giving nationalist leaders two principal instruments of rule: the party and the state bureaucracy. The party was supposed to be mass based, united and disciplined; yet, in reality it was often little more than 'a loose movement which naturally incorporated the characteristics of the society in which it grew' (Zolberg 1966, 123). The government, in contrast, was an alien institution, until recently run by Europeans according to strange bureaucratic norms. Nonetheless, it was the most concrete expression of central authority available. Given a huge shortage of trained and highly educated personnel within the party, many of the most capable loyalists were appointed to government, depriving the party of their skills and energy. Meanwhile, a deep-seated suspicion of government bureaucrats led to attempts to incorporate civil servants into the party. The outcome was predictable. The coherence of the party machinery and efficiency of the civil service both declined, while governmental structures became as salient as the parties. The accompanying trend towards centralisation of authority in the hands of the president led to his reliance upon lieutenants, some of whom owed their position to their background in the party and others having risen through the bureaucracy, but all, ultimately, owed their loyalty and legitimacy to their 'chief'. This hybrid pattern extended downwards through the party–government complex, so the lines of authority became confused and overlapping. The resulting contestation between party and state, the centre and the periphery, in groups and out groups and indeed between the president and his lieutenants was dependent on personal and political loyalties.

The study of political parties in Africa has moved by now beyond Zolberg's schema. Nonetheless, there is still considerable value to be drawn from his analysis when we consider the fate of NLMs in Southern Africa. First, the analysis of the development of the party-state, with its simultaneous strength (resting upon institutional foundations) and its fragility (incorporating the cleavages inherent in 'underdeveloped' societies), has strong parallels in Southern Africa, notably the shift from liberation movements to party dominance, albeit with such dominance rendered incomplete by the ruling party's own heterogeneity, internal contestations and (intermittent) practice of internal democracy. Second, Zolberg (and other students of the early nationalist parties) had the virtue of taking political parties seriously. Any perusal of those writings demonstrates that nationalist parties faced a multiplicity of challenges. Meeting them required a diversity of roles: what Tordoff (2002) (amongst others) referred to as their integrative, legitimising, policy, mobilisation and reconciliation, patronage and political communication functions.

Zolberg's analysis of West Africa's party states, therefore, serves as a fruitful starting point for interpreting the character of governance in post-apartheid South Africa, emphasising the ANC's successful adaptation to real-world challenges rather than its failure to conform to abstract, ideal-typical norms. Doubtless, there are important additional dimensions that must be taken into account. Such analysis tended to be divorced from wider considerations of national and international political economy, for example. In particular, it underplayed the emergence of new class structures, the transformation of ruling parties into agencies of class rule and the contradictions involved in countries where radical parties, themselves subject to such tendencies, were nonetheless simultaneously committed to socialist transformation. Certainly, at the time, experiments in one party democracy and African socialism were taken extremely seriously by radical analysts, most notably those concerned with the attempt to promote socialism in Tanzania (for example, Cliffe and Saul 1972). In a later era, Saul and others correctly emphasised the formidable battery of economic, political and cultural means western capitalism utilised to discipline African countries, but this does not justify a dismissive approach to former NLMs that are performing the political roles of their predecessors with varying degrees of success. The questions should be how are they performing, why and in whose interest?

So there is much to be said for focusing our analysis on the transformation of the nationalist (or liberation) movement into a party machine. It allows for an examination of the capacities of the NLM for undertaking those various *functions of the political party* emphasised by earlier scholars. In the South African context, it stresses the need to understand the capacity of the ANC to mobilise popular support, notably at election times, but intermittently at others, too. It invites analysis of the functioning of the ANC's structures in terms of control from above, participation from below and 'official' versus 'unofficial' lines of authority. It also, importantly, requires an understanding of how capacities to mobilise are underpinned by the raising and allocation of resources (the issue of party funding).

Second, it requires an analysis of *the role of the party in providing avenues of recruitment, advancement and social class formation*. In so doing, this allows for the possibility that the nature of the party may change over time, perhaps from being a vehicle of liberation to an instrument of political control and economic accumulation by an elite. This in turn implies the possibility of a shift in the function of the party from being an opponent towards becoming a collaborator with global capitalism. Third, it offers a concerted focus upon the party as a *machine for the allocation of positions, privileges, resources and contracts*. Perhaps this signifies a return to Eastonian notions of politics as the allocation of values, of who gets what, why and when, yet it also interlocks with Fanonist notions of the party as an instrument of class domination. Crucially, however, I would argue that because the party is operating within a context of resource scarcity, party relations with the state and with capital must be analysed, for they constitute the primary founts of resources.

Finally, resource scarcity – especially in post-colonial contexts of social inequality and widespread poverty – implies intra-party competition between 'ins' and 'outs', different components of the coalition the ruling party represents and between different segments of the political elite. I would suggest this points to the urgent necessity of 'network analysis', to identify groups of individuals linked together by bonds of interest (not exclusive of ideology) and their location within the party-state across level, region, class and ethnicity. In the contemporary context, such analysis demands that we search out cross-border linkages, forged between elements within the different liberation movements, between elites in different African countries and between political actors and international and African businesses.

Detailed probing of the ANC along these lines needs to be ambitious, involving not only pulling together much existent information but also drilling down into party structures, for most analysis hitherto has principally involved the ANC at the national level. In particular, we need to know much more about how the ANC works at provincial and local levels and the different social networks in which its elites participate and how and why they contest. There will be no serious attempt to undertake such a venture here, only to seek to illustrate this approach by brief reference to the ANC under Zuma.

The ANC as a party machine: from Mbeki to Zuma

The dominant party critique laments the ANC's failure to transform from a liberation movement into a political party and asserts its formation of a 'party-state'. By this it means the ANC has subverted the independence of state institutions, notably through the practice of 'deployment'. The implication is that the interests of the ANC ultimately will win out over those of the state. However, Zolberg's more nuanced presentation of the 'party-state' as a hybrid, in which the lines of authority become confused, and in which there is simultaneously contestation between party and state, provides a much more satisfactory description of developments in South Africa since 1994. To be sure, the practice of 'transformation' has been employed to secure the loyalty of key elements of the state machinery. However, the Mandela–Mbeki period was as much a period of intense struggle *between* the state and the party (for instance, the top–down imposition of GEAR) and *within* the party *about* the state (intense battles between left and right about economic policy), as it was one characterised by a steady imposition of ANC dominance *over* the state (via deployment). Thus, one of the primary motivations behind the campaign to defeat Mbeki's bid to secure re-election as ANC president was to reverse his imposition of a dictatorship and centralisation of authority; yet, whether this referred primarily to his role as party president or state president was never clear, perhaps precisely because they had become so confused.

Nonetheless, in retrospect the following can be said about the Zuma–Mbeki power struggle. First, Zuma's triumph represented something of a victory for constitutionalism. Mbeki's bid for a third term as party leader, even though, as dictated by the national constitution, he could not run for president again, implied Mbeki would seek to control his successor even after the next general election. His defeat led the two positions to be separated clearly, and while some complained that his ousting as state president in September 2008 represented the subversion of the constitution by the ANC, this particular coup had the hallmarks of liberal parliamentarism. Had Mbeki chosen to defy the party, he could have taken his case to Parliament, the only body that had the constitutional right to dismiss him. Yet he chose to resign because he appreciated that he would have been defeated if he had risked a vote of no confidence. Against this, of course, there is plentiful evidence that the contest between Zuma and Mbeki undermined the efficient functioning of the state machinery (notably the security services), leading to paralysis and illegality, and severely compromised the independence of legal institutions, notably the National Prosecuting Authority. Yet, the most important point is that it was Zuma's capture of the ANC machinery that was the determining factor in the struggle.

Under the ANC's constitution, the organisation's branches elect 90% of the voting delegates at the National Conference, which is charged with electing the party's president, other senior office holders and National Executive Committee (NEC). The remaining 10% come from provincial executives, the Women's and Youth League and other departments. If the ANC machinery had been controlled from above via Communist-style centralism, Mbeki presumably would have been re-elected smoothly. Although the ANC has pretended that campaigning for elective position does not take place within the party (leaders are said to emerge from the Rousseau-ian will of the people), the reality is that such campaigning does occur. Thus, those opposed to Mbeki realised that ousting him depended on securing control of sufficient party branches to secure election of an alternative candidate for party president and this, in essence, is what COSATU, the SACP and other elements of the pro-Zuma coalition achieved. At one level, it was undoubtedly internal democracy at work. Yet at another level, it indicated that control over the ANC party machinery trumped power over the state rather than the other way round (unlike in Zimbabwe, where Mugabe's party authority is now guaranteed by his control over the military). Zuma himself endorsed this position when he installed ANC deputy party leader Kgalema Motlanthe as interim state president after Mbeki's resignation. Recognising the intensity of the divisions within the ANC, he preferred to consolidate his position by attempting to neutralise the impact of the defection of Mbeki loyalists into the break-away Congress of the People (COPE) and by preparing the ground for the forthcoming election.

Mobilisation and legitimation

NLMs claim to represent the will of the nation; by implication, those opposing them are the enemy, divisive and illegitimate. The trope is one of anti-imperialist struggle, popular war and absolute victory, but the reality is rarely so uncomplicated, and certainly not in South Africa where political stalemate resulted in the compromises that led to the 1993 constitution. In such a circumstance, the ANC had to refigure its popular legitimacy by securing victory in the country's first democratic election. Thereafter, popular legitimacy had to be reconfirmed by successive triumphs at five-year intervals. It was Zuma's great fortune that his struggle with Mbeki had little impact on the party's remarkable capacity to mobilise to win elections.

The continuing divisions within the ANC after Polokwane and their eruption into the formation of COPE led to predictions that the ANC's share of the popular vote might fall considerably from the high level it obtained in 2004 (69.7%). However, the ANC's organisational structures remained strong even between elections, and this was demonstrated effectively in the 2009 campaign, which was bolstered by the high degree of mobilisation that had taken place prior to Polokwane. The ANC's campaign did not appear to be hampered by the defection of activists to COPE and was coordinated effectively from party headquarters, with strong election teams set up at provincial and regional levels, and local branches assuming the burden of intensive house-to-house canvassing. COSATU and the SACP contributed substantial human and organisational resources, supplemented by vigorous campaigning by the Youth League and networks of veterans of the ANC's former military arm (the Umkhonto we Sizwe [MK]), and Zuma went out of his way to appeal to wide sectors of society, from the churches, to youth, minority groupings, business and so on. In short, the ANC demonstrated it had lost nothing of its capacity to mobilise the vote, despite having just gone through a major internal upheaval. The ANC suffered a few set-backs – it lost the Western Cape provincial election (the one province in the country where its organisation had been reduced to a shambles by infighting), its proportion of the vote fell in every province except KwaZulu-Natal (where the Zuma factor was particularly influential) and its share of the national vote was reduced to 65.9% – nonetheless, the extent of its victory was undeniably impressive (Butler 2009).

It is also clear that the ANC's repeat victory reflected its capacity to raise money. Parties in South Africa receive official state funding according to the level of their representation in parliament. This is widely recognised as insufficient to cover the expense of a major party's national organisation, much less the costs of its running an election campaign, so it is forced to seek additional funding elsewhere. Unquestionably, this had led to major controversies in the ANC, ranging from suggestions that an array of corporate donors have been induced to contribute to party coffers for fear they will operate at a disadvantage if they do not (with the implied promise they will secure an advantage if they do), to allegations that the ANC has received considerable funds from businesspersons involved in corrupt dealings or from its own covert plundering of state funds. In addition, strong suspicions have been registered that the ANC's own involvement in business represents a concerted attempt to direct state funding towards ANC-related entities via allocation of contracts by government departments and parastatals, notably through the investment trust Chancellor House Holdings. When Helen Zille, leader of the DA, registered objections to the World Bank's April 2010 loan for the construction of Medupi coal-fired power station, which was to be built in part by Hitachi, a firm in which Chancellor House has a 25% shareholding, they were made on the grounds that it would divert substantial funds into ANC coffers. Although subsequent to the World Bank loan agreement, the ANC debated whether Chancellor should divest itself of its interest, there was no wider commitment to reducing its involvement in business deals that are ultimately reliant upon state money. Notwithstanding these debates over the source of ANC funds, combined with gifts the ANC appeared to receive from foreign sources (governments, ruling parties and potential investors), there is little question the ANC is massively albeit dubiously resourced (Southall 2008). Thus, Butler (2009, 73–74) indicates that the cost of the ANC's 2004 election campaign may have amounted to R300 million, while the one in 2009 was probably R400 to R500 million. Related estimates for expenditure by opposition parties are not available, but it is unlikely that they amounted to half of that, even in total. If the first job of a ruling party is to reproduce itself in power, then the ANC's capacity to use state power to fund the party is crucial and it has been successful.

Policy determination and intra-party competition

Competing political parties are expected to represent competing policies, and intra-party pressure groups or tendencies are similarly expected to congregate around alternatives. One of the major interpretations of Zuma's triumph over Mbeki was that it was a left takeover of the party by COSATU and the SACP. This is an exaggeration, as the support behind Zuma constituted a much wider coalition, but the left nonetheless has recorded advances on both the policy front and in its presence in government. At the cabinet level, the most significant changes have been the move of Trevor Manuel (the left's particular *bête noire*) from Finance to a new Ministry of Planning and his replacement by Pravin Gordhan, who served as a member of the SACP's central committee in exile (Gordhan also shared a connection with Zuma through ANC intelligence operations, and established a reputation for ruthless efficiency as head of the South African Revenue Service under Mbeki). In addition, Zuma appointed Ebrahim Patel, previously general secretary of COSATU's textile workers' union, to head a new Ministry of Economic Development; the SACP's Rob Davies as Minister of Trade and Industry, and Blade Nzimande, general secretary of the SACP, as Minister of Higher Education. Together, these appointments implied a shift of power away from the Ministry of Finance and the Treasury towards pro-planning ministers and the adoption of more statist economic policies.

The left has wanted the government to become more active in restructuring the economy, countering the de-industrialisation caused by former government's liberalisation policies (designed to render industries more globally competitive) and introducing policies that will reduce the country's dismal level of unemployment. The main proposal has been to move away from high levels of dependence on minerals export towards increased minerals beneficiation (minerals processing and development of related industries including equipment and engineering) and expansion of industry. In practice, however, the outcome has been an uncertain victory for the left. The move towards a more active industrial policy was embodied in the government's adoption of the new Industrial Policy Action Plan (IPAP) 2010/11-2012/2013, presented to parliament in February 2010. Now in its sixth iteration, the initial IPAP pledged to support to 12 sectors of the economy and promised to create 2.4 million 'decent' jobs over 10 years. It placed manufacturing at the heart of its strategy, arguing that development of 'value-added' sectors will allow 'service' sectors to grow. While the plan pledged R8.2 billion over the first three years, funding was slow to be obtained for full implementation of the strategy. Furthermore, as Paton notes, while it placed emphasis upon expansion of infrastructure, provision of concessional finance by the Industrial Development Corporation and expansion of the capital equipment sector through government procurement, it is questionable whether it can replicate the experience of successful 'developmental states' upon which it is modelled (*Financial Mail*, 26 February 2010). Demonstrable weaknesses in state capacity are complicated by ideological differences and the problem of corruption, the core of which is located in state procurement processes via the allocation of tenders.

At the time the IPAP was being introduced to parliament, there were three broad tendencies evident within the ANC. The first was represented by those who prioritised the need for macro-economic stability (controlling inflation, deficits and the value of the currency). They were centred in the Ministry of Finance and the Treasury, then under Gordhan. The second was the broad left, which favours redistribution and the 'developmental state'. They were centred in the ANC–COSATU–SACP Alliance and located in the Department of Trade and Industry and Economic Planning. The third had strong links to business and is heavily dependent upon Black Economic Empowerment programmes (BEE), procurement and patronage. By its nature, this third grouping has tended to be more diffuse and more opportunistic, with instrumental forays into ideological battle.

Tensions among these three groupings became wide open under Zuma, for if his presidential head tells him to follow the first tendency, he is heavily obligated to the second, and yet his material interests would appear to lie very much with the third. His penchant has been for appeasement rather than resolution of differences, so his public stance has tended to reflect the audience he is addressing, thus satisfying no one. The result has been increasing division within the party and the wider Alliance, and confusion over policy direction. For instance, during a visit to London in March 2010, he gave assurances that the government would maintain its present commitments to macro-economic stability, immediately landing himself in hot water with COSATU for his allegedly pro-business stance. COSATU was further outraged that the ANC rejected its own call to rid the party of corrupt leaders by implementing 'lifestyle audits'.

Zuma proved equally inept in dealing with maverick ANC Youth League (ANCYL) leader Julius Malema, whose most controversial policy proposal was a strong call for the nationalisation of the mines. According to the ANCYL, nationalisation of the mines should become ANC policy to ensure democratised control of mining assets as outlined by the Freedom Charter and should be achieved by expropriation and levels of compensation dependent upon individual mines' profitability. Talk of nationalisation sent jitters down the back of capital, forcing Zuma to calm the waters internationally and domestically by indicating, variously, that nationalisation was not policy or that it was merely a matter for debate. Malema's noisy punting of his proposal was accompanied by the release of an official initiative by the Department of Rural Development and Land Reform to nationalise all farmland (via the introduction of a quitrent land tenure system which would limit individual ownership rights). This was immediately backed by the Youth League, giving rise to alarmist concerns that South Africa was on the verge of emulating Zimbabwe, a perception soon reinforced by a hugely publicised visit to that country by Malema, where, in comradely meetings with the ZANU-PF Youth League, he sang the praises of Mugabe, his land seizures and his party's plans for 'indigenisation' of capital.

An assertive leadership would have brought Malema swiftly to heel, especially given his other antics that had already deeply embarrassed segments of the ANC. As it was, Zuma sought to rein him in only after his visit to Zimbabwe, which coincided with the brutal murder of Eugene Terreblanche, the leader of the right wing Afrikaner Resistance Movement (Afrikaner Weerstandsbeweging [AWB]). Many whites ascribed the attack directly or indirectly to Malema's resurrection of the struggle song 'Kill the Boer', and Terreblanche's demise certainly damaged South Africa's image of racial reconciliation and stability. Yet more than denting Zuma's authority, Malema's populist call for nationalisation also enraged and confused the left. The leadership of the SACP had effectively abandoned the call for nationalisation in the early 1990s, subsequently calling for strategic state intervention via the 'developmental state', but never had the courage to eliminate nationalisation from its programme, preferring to hide behind ambiguous formulations about 'democratic socialism'. The ANCYL proposals sparked tensions within the SACP on this unresolved issue.

When examined in detail, Malema's favoured proposal was for a new state mining holding company in which private capital would be forced into partnerships with black mining companies, which Butler (*Business Day*, 8 March 2010) has termed a strategy for a 'corporate welfare system for overleveraged and politically connected miners' and an opportunity for the industry to dump exhausted mines on to the state. These proposals were not very different from an idea emanating from the Department of Minerals that envisaged creation of a state mining sector, backed by the Public Investment Corporation, the custodian of public sector pension funds, a programme openly supported by Patel, although opposed by Gordhan and the National Treasury. As Butler suggests, whereas the left might rationally have been expected to back the attempts of the latter to clamp down on the looting of state coffers, it now found its own developmental initiatives put them in much the same camp as those who feed on patronage (*Business Day*, 29 March 2010). In short, a potentially constructive policy debate between the relative merits of macro-economic stability and developmentalism, and a potential alliance between right and left to clamp down on corruption, is in danger of falling victim to the private ambitions of those who view connection to party and state as the route to wealth.

Patronage and the allocation of resources

A widespread impression, shared by critics within and outside the party, is that the ANC has descended into a morass of cronyism and corruption, exemplifying the worst fears of Fanon. The roots of this degeneration are said to lie in the notorious arms deal (whereby multinational arms companies passed huge sums to connected individuals and probably to the party itself), de-ideologisation of the struggle due to the compromise of the transition, aspirations to wealth and upward class mobility by party members and notions of racial entitlement fed by the strategies of affirmative action and the political cronyism that have accompanied BEE. Key to all developments has been the ANC's capture of the state at all levels – national, provincial and local – creating opportunities to allocate positions, procurements and privileges to party loyalists and those connected with them. The public was already aware of the cancerous growth of patronage and corruption under Mbeki. They are convinced that if anything, the rot has become worse under Zuma.

That should not be so surprising, because Zuma's struggle for the Presidency was inextricably intertwined with his battle to avoid prosecution for having accepted bribes in connection with the arms deal. Furthermore, there is substantial reason to believe that his rise to the top was backed by elements within the party who either had been marginalised by Mbeki or who had been unable to secure benefits. Thus, countless numbers of those seeking to retain or gain access to power and wealth via state connections jumped on his bandwagon. The outcome has been vicious struggles at different levels within the party both before and long after the election and a widespread sense of invulnerability that has been buttressed, inter alia, by Zuma's careful placing of a personal loyalist, Menzi Simelane, into the position of Public Prosecutor. Simelane, in turn, has used his position to eliminate any lingering prospect that the president will be prosecuted or that there will be an enquiry into the arms deal.

Of all the dubious developments that provide constant fodder to the independent (not the state-owned) media, three stand out. The first concerns the activities of Zuma's own entourage. All four of Zuma's wives are entitled to financial and logistical support from the state as presidential spouses, with other benefits extending to his dependent children. According to the article on spousal support in the *Mail & Guardian* on 17 March 2010, the cost of this has nearly doubled from R8.1 in 2008–2009 to R15.5 million in 2009–2010. More significant is the Zuma family's determined push into business. A recent exposé indicated that of 16 adults – wives, lovers and children – who can be linked to Zuma, 15 are in business, and together with the president account for 134 company directorships or memberships in privately held corporations. Eighty-three of the companies have been registered since Polokwane; together, the Zuma-connected companies range across property, mining, trade, telecommunications and information technology. Not all these companies are active, but most are, and while not all are trading with the government, questions have been raised about the allocation of state contracts to a number of them. There is further evidence that 'political entrepreneurs' are fostering connections with the Zuma family, some of them to secure a smooth transition between the Mbeki and Zuma eras. One wealthy businessman (backed by others) bailed out Zuma's second wife when she was threatened with eviction from a Durban mansion for non-payment of rent, while others hastened to appoint Zuma relatives to their boards (*Mail & Guardian*, 19–25 March 2010). As Zuma would hasten to say, none of the family-related firms has been proven to be corrupt, yet the impression is that these businesses expect to gain from 'political connectivity'. Certainly, Sizana Dlamini-Dubuzana, who bought a house in Johannesburg for Zuma's use after he was removed from the deputy presidency in 2005 (and has declined to state whether he paid rent), subsequently benefited from loans to her hotel company from KwaZulu-Natal's Ithala Development Corporation, which at the time answered to provincial Finance Minister Zwele Mkhize, a close Zuma ally (*Mail & Guardian*, 19–25 March 2010).

Reports also surfaced that Communications Minister Siphiwe Nyanda, former head of the defence force, owns a 50% stake in General Nyanda Security (GNS) Risk Advisory Services (later named Abalozi Security Risk Advisory Services), which has received multi-million Rand contracts from state agencies without having followed proper tendering processes. One involved the allocation of R55 million by Transnet Freight Services; another saw a R67.8 million contract awarded by Gauteng Department of roads and transport. Although Nyanda resigned his directorship of GNS and located his shares in a family trust, allegations are rife that he has used his political connections to huge personal advantage. This impression was not dispelled by his public backing for Siyabonga Gama, who presided over Transnet Freight at the time of the award, and who was subsequently suspended but cried foul when he was passed over for appointment as Chief Executive of Transnet's entire operation. While Abalozi is seeking to have the finding of a Transnet disciplinary committee that the GNS contract was fraudulently awarded overturned, Nyanda continued to sit in cabinet (*Mail & Guardian*, 29 January 2010).

Finally, reference has to be made yet again to Julius Malema, who, whilst publicly playing the buffoon, has seemingly achieved considerable wealth by mysterious means to fund an ostentatious lifestyle. Malema's good fortune appears to rest on his political connections in Limpopo, his home province, where he has highly placed friends. Malema has been linked to four companies that have benefited from tenders awarded by the Limpopo Government. One of them, SGL Engineering, benefited from contracts worth over R140 million. Malema has either denied being, or claims to have resigned, as a director; however, Cipro (the government's companies' register) lists him as director of all four companies. Meanwhile, suspicions have been aired that he has connections to mining companies investing in Zimbabwe, and that he is transferring money out of South Africa in order to escape media scrutiny. Whatever the source of his wealth, it has embroiled him in vicious battles with the left, which has called for his lifestyle to be audited by South African Revenue Services. Malema responded by accusing the left, the media and SARS itself for plotting against him and other leading figures supportive of Zuma. Needless to say, as noted in the article Malema's War, ANC executive members have come out against the idea of lifestyle audits as discriminatory, and driven by forces with 'political agendas' (*Mail & Guardian*, 26 February 2010).

In response to revelations such as these, the ANC has vowed to tighten up legislation concerning conflicts of interest and disclosures of politicians, and generally to make war on corruption. Yet extensive legislation is already in place, and what is systematically lacking is implementation and prosecution. For instance, a register established in 2005 to list companies found guilty of tender fraud has remained blank. Veteran journalist Allister Sparks (*Business Day*, April 14, 2010) is not alone in suggesting the ANC has reached a corruption deadlock, where people in high places have so much dirt on each other that no one dares to blow the whistle. More relevant than that for our purposes, there are networks of influence that would reveal shared interests linking the politically connected across sector, the Alliance, provincial and (almost certainly) international boundaries in Southern Africa. It is the ANC that holds all this together.[4]

Conclusion: towards reform of the machine?

Despite its sometimes dubious practices as a political party, the ANC retains considerable reserves of idealism and commitment to realising the historic goals of the liberation movement, non-racialism and a better life for all. Nor is there any shortage of analysis within the party about what is going wrong. In a recent discussion paper, Febe Potgieter, a member of the party's NEC, raises a series of concerns about developments within the party in the years since the democratic transition, as raised particularly by the leadership struggle at Polokwane.

Noting that open contestation for the party leadership had been fundamental to the ANC before its banning in 1960, Potgieter argues that this organisational culture was subverted after 1990 by the challenge of integrating the party with the internal mass democratic movement, re-establishing legal structures across the country, and uniting different generations who had engaged in the struggle. Furthermore, the movement of experienced cadres to government left a vacuum at party headquarters and had a deleterious impact on mass organisation. Thus, in successive ANC conferences, concerns have been raised about how the movement has become subject to divisive tendencies as individuals have come to see leadership positions as stepping stones to power and material reward. Thus, the *Strategy and Tactics* document adopted in 1997 expressed worry about the ANC emulating the tendencies of liberation movements and their leaderships that had become distant from their mass constituencies once they achieved power. As well, an ANC National General Council meeting in 2000 identified disturbing trends of careerism, corruption and opportunism in the party. By 2002, such battles over access to resources and patronage, and allegations about corruption linked to the business interests of leadership, had become 'more of a generalised trend', entrenched by growing intolerance for debate, use of violence to resolve disagreements, indecent behaviour, name-calling and covert lobbying. Such developments represent 'a shadow culture which coexists alongside what the movement always stood for', and like a parasite, use the democratic structures of the movement for its own ends.

Despite this shadow, Potgieter insists that the ANC has achieved much under difficult historical circumstances, with the 2009 election showing that despite facing a split from within, 'the ANC as a political movement still has the greatest capacity for uniting and mobilising the country behind a common vision'. Consequently, as resolved by the Polokwane Conference, there is an urgent need for organisational renewal. How, then, to confront patronage and neo-patrimonialism, bureaucratisation, corruption and erosion of progressive values and organisational culture? Suffice to say that along with recommendations such as the introduction of firm guidelines about party funding, she urges the ANC to draw clear lines between right and wrong, strengthen internal election procedures, introduce rules on lobbying, discipline misconduct, develop leadership capabilities through political education and, above all, build a new morality and a new cadreship oriented to reshaping existing social relations and engendering new social values (Potgieter-Gqubule 2010).

The broad thrust of Potgieter's analysis has been taken up in a paper on 'Leadership renewal, discipline and organisational culture', which was prepared for the ANC's National General Council, a body that meets between National Congresses and discusses issues and policy. Inter alia, it notes that disturbing trends of 'careerism, corruption and opportunism' have taken root within the contemporary ANC, 'eating our soul' and eroding the party's capacity to be an agent of social change. Worse, it notes that there has been a disturbing growth of factionalism, use of violence against competing factions, intolerance of debate, unruly behaviour at meetings, purges and, notably, the influence and use of money as an aspect of lobbying for organisational positions. It calls for a 'battle of renewal' featuring renewed emphasis upon the 'value system of a national democratic society', the exercising of political and state power in the interest of the people, an assault upon factionalism and intolerance, enforcement of rules to ensure the integrity of internal elections, the development of rules on lobbying, enforcement of such and finally upon the use of branches and the Youth and Women's leagues as 'political schools' and upon the institutionalisation of a 'leadership and cadre policy' (African National Congress 2010).

It would seem those within the ANC who lament its present trajectory will back Potgieter's vision for organisational renewal, and indeed, she cites Zuma as sharing it. However, many will ask whether such a project is viable under a man whose rise to the Presidency was backed by the very social forces Potgieter condemns, and who, at present, appears to lack both the capacity and will to control them. Our analysis here has emphasised the contradictions internal to the ANC – its ability to reproduce its dominance by winning elections while simultaneously being at war with itself over policy and patronage – may provide part of the answer. Such contradictions are part and parcel of its evolution and development as a party machine and will continue to shape the party in the years to come.

The evidence and analysis presented in this article have suggested that the ruling ANC has moved considerably in the direction of transforming from an NLM to a political party typical of a developing country context. As I have shown, current debates within the ANC indicate that neither the *dominant party* approach, which assumes the ANC conforms to the ideological, centralist and authoritarian model of NLMs, which impede democracy, nor the *Fanonesque* perspective, which claims the ANC has lost its transformative ideology (but not its centralist or authoritarian character), are wholly satisfactory. Using the example of the recent struggles in the party associated with Zuma's rise to leadership, I have shown that it is more analytically helpful to take the ANC seriously as a political party, facing the multiplicity of challenges similar parties face in developing the capacity to rule by mobilising to secure electoral support; offering avenues of recruitment, advancement and social class formation and allocating privileges. Inevitably, in a post-colonial context, one will see intra-party competition between 'ins' and 'outs,' which indeed served as the impetus for the Mbeki-Zuma conflict and the subsequent debates about corruption under Zuma's leadership. Although this paper was only able to begin the detailed probing of the ANC along these lines needed, it has illustrated some of the advantages of this approach in understanding the nature of South African democracy under the ANC.

Notes

1. Jacob Zuma is president of the ANC and became president of South Africa in 2009, following the ANC's victory in the country's general elections. He was re-elected in the May 2014 general elections. This paper was written after the 2009 elections, and focuses on the ANC under Zuma during his first term in office, especially the first few years of his presidency. As such, the paper does not take into account recent developments in the country; however, an assessment of post-2013 developments would not really affect the thrust of the analysis.
2. The title of Leon Trotsky's 1936 denunciation of the Soviet Union under Stalin.
3. A reference to the US Democratic Party political machine which controlled Manhattan from 1854 to 1932 through a mix of strong arm tactics, patronage and corruption
4. Forde notes in the Star article on 25 February 2010 key networks include those connected through Operation Vula, this playing an influential but shadowy role in the elevation of Zuma. A network crossing Vula and Alliance lines involves a linkage between the Zuma's second wife, Nompumelo Ntuli, and Noluthando Vavi, wife of COSATU General Secretary Zwelinzama Vavi, who share interests in a property registered in the name of Vivian Reddy, a main financial backer of Zuma with close connections to those involved in Operation Vula.

References

African National Congress. 2010. "Leadership Renewal, Discipline and Organisational Culture." Discussion paper for the National General Council, *ANC*. September 20–24.

Bond, Patrick. 1998. *Elite Transition: From Neo-Apartheid to Neo-Liberalism in South Africa*. London: Pluto Press.

Butler, Anthony. 2009. "The ANC's National Election Campaign of 2009: Siyanqoba!" In *Zunami! The 2009 South African Elections*, edited by Roger Southall and John Daniel, 65–84. Johannesburg: Jacana.

Cliffe, Lionel, and John S. Saul, eds. 1972. *Socialism in Tanzania: An Interdisciplinary Reader. Vol. 1. Politics*. Nairobi: East African Publishing House.

Dangerfield, George. 1997. *The Strange Death of Liberal England*. Stanford, CA: Stanford University Press. [First published 1935.]

Fanon, Frantz. 1974. *The Wretched of the Earth*. London: Penguin. [First published 1961.]

Giliomee, Hermann, and Charles Simkins, eds. 1999. *The Awkward Embrace: One Party Domination and Democracy*. Cape Town: Tafelberg.

Giliomee, Hermann, James Myburgh, and Lawrence Schlemmer. 2001. "Dominant Party Rule, Opposition Politics and Minorities in South Africa." In *Opposition and Democracy in South Africa*, edited by Roger Southall, 161–182. London: Frank Cass.

Melber, Henning. 2007. "Poverty, Politics, Power and Privilege: Namibia's Black Economic Elite Formation." In *Transitions in Namibia: Which Changes for Whom?*, edited by Henning Melber, 110–129. Uppsala: The Nordic Africa Institute.

Pempel, T. F., ed. 1990. *Uncommon Democracies*. Ithaca, NY: Cornell University Press.

Potgieter-Gqubule, Febe. 2010. "Through the Eye of the Needle: Elections, Lobbying and Leadership Transition in the ANC." *Umrabulo* 32 (1st Quarter). www.ancorg.za/shiw.php?doc=ancdocs/pubs/umrabulo/umrabulo32/art8.html.

Saul, John S. 2008. *Decolonization and Empire*. London: Merlin. www.ancorg.za/shiw.php?doc=ancdocs/pubs/umrabulo/umrabulo32/art8.html.

Southall, Roger. 2001. "Conclusion: Emergent Perspectives on Opposition in South Africa." In *Opposition and Democracy in South Africa*, edited by Roger Southall, 275–284. London: Frank Cass.

Southall, Roger. 2005. "The 'Dominant Party Debate' in South Africa." *Afrika Spectrum* 1: 61–82.

Southall, Roger. 2008. "Thabo Mbeki's Fall: the ANC and South Africa's Democracy." *Open Democracy*. Accessed October 14. http://www.opendemocracy.net/article/thabo-mbekis-fall-the-anc-and-south-africas-democracy.

Southall, Roger. 2009. "Understanding the 'Zuma Tsunami'." *Review of African Political Economy* 36 (121): 317–333. doi:10.1080/03056240903210739.

Tordoff, William. 2002. *Government and Politics in Africa*, 4th ed. Bloomington: University of Indiana Press.

Zolberg, Aristide. 1966. *Creating Political Order: The Party States of West Africa*. Chicago, IL: Rand McNally.

A parallel universe – competing interpretations of Zimbabwe's crisis[1]

Linda Freeman

Department of Political Science, Carleton University, Ottawa, ON, Canada

This article examines competing interpretations of the nature and cause of Zimbabwe's contemporary crisis. It finds that while neoliberal macroeconomic policies promoted by international financial institutions helped to provide a structural basis for the crisis, arguments attributing blame to Britain and to wider Western sanctions are overblown and inaccurate. Similarly, although Western reactions to Zimbabwe's land reform have had a racist tinge, these paled in comparison with the explicit racist intent of policies adopted by the Zimbabwean Government. The claim that Zimbabwe is undergoing a process of progressive transformation must be weighed against the nature of state power, the intensification of class divisions, a precipitous economic decline, a problematic development strategy and the extreme abuse of human, civil and political rights.

The struggle within Zimbabwe during the 2000s has been accompanied by a vigorous debate over the nature of liberation movements in power and the prospects for a new form of politics in Southern Africa. Lined up on one side have been those stressing continuity with the past, insisting that the terrain and *dramatis personae* have not changed, that the battle is only the latest chapter of the struggle which brought Zimbabwe to independence (Mamdani 2008; Moyo and Yeros 2005, 2007; Yeros 2002). A central proposition of the opposing position is that the current crisis is less about completing the final stages of Zimbabwean liberation than a reaction by the Zimbabwe African National Union Patriotic Front (ZANU-PF) to the most serious challenge to its power since independence (Concerned Africa Scholars 2009; Raftopoulos 2006; Moore 2004; Raftopoulos and Phimister 2004; Bond and Manyanya 2002). In sum, the first approach puts an emphasis on external factors and regards President Robert Mugabe as leading a vanguard for national sovereignty and revolutionary transformation. The second focuses more on internal dynamics – the nature of ZANU-PF in power and its determination to exclude opposition forces.

This article will review these competing interpretations. It will argue that, while neoliberal macroeconomic policies promoted by international financial institutions (IFIs) helped to provide a structural basis for the crisis, arguments attributing blame to Britain and to wider Western sanctions are overblown and inaccurate. Similarly, although Western reactions to Zimbabwe's land reform have had a racist tinge, these paled in comparison with the explicit racist intent of policies adopted by the Zimbabwean

Government. There is no question that policies of national ownership and affirmative action have not only produced a major redistribution of land to small farmers, but they have also served as the basis for a massive programme of patronage for the power elite. Finally, the claim that Zimbabwe is undergoing a process of progressive transformation will be weighed against the nature of state power, the intensification of class divisions, a precipitous economic decline, a problematic development strategy and the extreme abuse of human, civil and political rights.

Mugabe, ZANU-PF and the revolutionary project

In the first case, those who support and defend the transformation wrought by ZANU-PF since 2000 invoke the continuity of revolutionary tradition (see Mamdani 2008; Moyo and Yeros 2007). The claim is that, in its attempt to return ownership of Zimbabwe's productive base to the African majority, the ZANU-PF state is finishing the tasks of the liberation struggle. The theoretical provenance is almost entirely structuralist and historicist, employing the grand narratives of anti-colonialism, imperialism and even socialism. These link the present crisis to the battle against white minority rule that ended with independence in 1980 and the larger battle of the South against domination by international capital and the advanced industrial world.

This explanation of the Zimbabwean crisis has five main dimensions endorsed primarily by those within the ZANU-PF camp[2]: that land reform has been misconstrued by racist opponents; that the structural adjustment policies the government was persuaded to adopt by donors and IFIs in the early 1990s provide the larger context for the crisis in the 2000s; that the crisis is primarily the fault of Britain and other Western powers; that the rise of an opposition force in the Movement for Democratic Change (MDC) represents a backlash from the wealthy white farming sector and its external supporters; and that citizenship belongs primarily to those who back ZANU-PF. Let us examine each of these points in turn.

The central point of land reform in this perspective is to end racial inequality in landownership and to pave the way for redistribution in other sectors of the economy. Zimbabwean development had been blocked by the racial imbalance which two decades after independence saw a tiny number of white commercial farmers (about 4500) still owning almost 70% of the best farmland while nearly 7 million African farmers operated in conditions of extreme overcrowding and land shortage in communal areas. The latter farms were located in the driest regions with the worst soils, while white-owned commercial farmers held vast tracts of unutilised arable land (Elich 2005). Following the completion of the land reform in 2009, resettlement farmers occupied 26.8% of the land while the share of large-scale commercial growers was reduced to 6% (Hawkins 2012).

Above all, then, land reforms rectified a major historical injustice, recapturing land that had been stolen during the process of white settlement. Proponents argued that receiving stolen property, innocently or not, gives no claim on it and no right to compensation for losses under the law. Hence, in this view, there was no need to pay for this land; only for improvements to farms. In any case, Mugabe made clear that his government would brush aside legal impediments: 'The courts can do whatever they want', he said, 'but no judicial decision will stand in our way' (Zimbabwe Human Rights NGO Forum and the Justice for Agriculture Trust in Zimbabwe 2007, 13–14). At ZANU-PF's insistence, the new 2013 constitution explicitly prohibits a legal challenge to land expropriation by the state. Suggestions that land reform is responsible for the decline in agricultural production are said to be premature at best and untrue and racist at worst. While incomes may decline in the present, redistributing land will lay the basis for a more egalitarian income generation and distribution in the future. Indeed, a recent school of thought argues that there are clear signs of a rebound in production and the emergence of a successful smallholder sector located on the land which has been redistributed (Scoones et al. 2010; Hanlon, Manjengwa, and Smart 2013).

Rather than the economic crisis having been caused by land redistribution, in this view, Zimbabwe has been punished by Western powers and institutions for stepping out of line. In the 1990s, the Zimbabwean Government had adopted and then refused to continue the standard neoliberal recipe of downsizing the state, privatising state companies, deregulating and liberalising. By the late 1990s, the government abandoned this programme when the results proved economically disappointing and politically disastrous. Shortly after, IFIs retaliated, stopping balance of payments support and other financial assistance. Even after the government repaid a substantial part of its arrears, the IFIs did not resume funding.

This cut-off added to already fraught relations with the West. In the view of the Mugabe Government, Britain and to a lesser extent the USA had reneged on promises made at the Lancaster House Conference in 1979 to fund a major land redistribution programme as part of the negotiation process that brought Zimbabwe to independence. When the Zimbabwean Government proceeded with its programme of fast-track land reform, Western countries imposed what are regarded as illegal sanctions on Zimbabwe and actively plotted ways to unseat the Mugabe Government.

Until recently, these sanctions prohibited Mugabe and more than 200 senior members of his regime from travelling to Europe, the USA, Australia, New Zealand and Canada and froze their financial assets. The European Union (EU) ceased military cooperation with Zimbabwe, banning arms sales, and would not allow 40 companies linked to the Mugabe regime to conduct business in EU countries. In 2001, the USA passed the Zimbabwe Democracy and Economic Recovery Act (ZDERA) which limited economic relations between US citizens and any person or entity considered responsible for undermining democratic institutions and processes in Zimbabwe. ZDERA also instructed US delegates to multilateral financial institutions to vote against financial aid to Zimbabwe and excluded Zimbabwe from the African Growth and Opportunity Act facility.

Beyond these measures, a regime of informal sanctions has been in effect since the beginning of the current crisis, with official aid frozen and lines of offshore credit cut by bilateral as well as multilateral donors. In particular, Western governments did not provide assistance to farmers who gained land under the reform. Private foreign investment from the West declined dramatically. Therefore, in this view, Zimbabwe was starved of foreign support as punishment for its confiscation of land from white farmers and its adoption of heterodox economic policies. Once in place, sanctions provided a strong deterrent for outside engagement of any sort. One report claimed Zimbabwe's losses from sanctions since 2001 amounted to $42 billion (*The Herald*, 10 July 2013).

Based on this analysis, the choice between ZANU-PF and the MDC is considered to be a choice between the party that brought Zimbabwe to independence and a reversion to domination by former colonial and current neocolonial forces. In Mugabe's words:

> The MDC … is immovably and implacably moored in the colonial yesteryear and embraces wittingly or unwittingly the repulsive ideology of return to white settler rule. MDC is as old

and as strong as the forces that control it. ...It is a counter revolutionary Trojan horse contrived and nurtured by the very inimical forces that enslaved and oppressed our people yesterday. (Raftopoulos 2005, 3)

From this perspective, the MDC represents an illegitimate, unAfrican and treasonous force, and ZANU-PF remains the sole legitimate heir to the liberation struggle. Attacks on MDC officials and supporters by groups aligned with ZANU-PF are justified as a means to prevent the return of Zimbabwe to neocolonial subjugation through the aegis of 'sell outs'. Political participation is considered to be the exclusive right of those within the ruling party. Hence, the MDC's election victory in 2008 was regarded as a temporary aberration, one that ZANU-PF went all out to reverse in the 2013 election. Questions of democratic space, liberties and human rights are depicted as irrelevant or counter-revolutionary. The existence of opposition forces is considered to be an affront; their activities understood as subversive attempts at regime change.

Citizenship, then, is defined selectively. Only peasant backers of ZANU-PF, especially in the rural areas of Mashonaland, are considered to be authentic citizens while large groups of Zimbabweans – urban dwellers, farm workers and whites – are not given status. ZANU-PF leader Didymus Mutasa went so far as to argue that, 'We would be better off with only 6 million people in Zimbabwe. They would be our own people who support the liberation struggle. We don't want all these extra people' (*The Scotsman*, 19 June 2005). Urban dwellers are dismissed as deracinated, totemless,[3] and at the periphery of the liberation legacy. The government termed a campaign to evict people in informal settlements in and around urban areas Operation Murambatsvina, which literally translated means to 'drive out the rubbish'. As Police Commissioner Augustine Chihuri put it, the Operation was meant to 'clean the country of the crawling mass of maggots bent on destroying the economy' (Ncube, Bate, and Tren 2005, 2).

Unlike peasants, farm workers are not viewed as true citizens either, in this case because many are descendants of migrant workers from Malawi, Mozambique and Zambia. ZANU-PF used their origins as an excuse to treat the entire group of farm workers as aliens without rights to land (Research and Advocacy Unit and Justice for Agriculture Trust 2009, 9–12). On similar grounds, white Zimbabweans, especially white farmers, were not accepted either. Addressing the ZANU-PF Congress in December 2009, Mugabe declared that 'this is your country and not for whites. They are settlers; even if they were born here, they are offspring of settlers' (*Zimbabwe Independent*, 4 September 2009).

In sum, the first approach regards President Robert Mugabe as conducting a revolutionary programme of transformation. For this camp, the key issue (indeed, the only issue) in understanding Zimbabwe's troubles is the refusal of forces within and without Zimbabwe to accept the radical reform that transferred commercial farmland from white to African farmers and then insisted on at least 51% ownership of other productive sectors of the economy. Hence, concern about the abuse of human, civil and political rights is considered to be a smokescreen to cover efforts to drive ZANU-PF from power and to put old enemies in its place. Those who find ZANU-PF's approach unpalatable are regarded as being part of a fresh imperialist project. In this view, Mugabe and his associates need to be celebrated for having completed an important task which had been integral to the liberation struggle.

Maintaining power at all costs

An alternative approach to understanding Zimbabwe's difficulties came into focus at the end of the 1990s (especially after 1997) as socio-economic problems, political repression and corruption mounted. Its central proposition is that the current crisis is the product of ZANU-PF's struggle to maintain power at all costs. In this view, ZANU-PF's refusal to accept the popular will has been demonstrated in the rigging of every parliamentary and presidential election since 2000, including the most recent election in 2013.

This perspective is based on five principal propositions: that the crisis is a product of ZANU-PF's attempts to shore up an eroding power base; that ZANU-PF promotes a non-liberal form of politics which has become highly abusive; that land reform has had, primarily, a political agenda; that external forces, especially IFIs and Britain, are not primarily responsible for the current state of Zimbabwe; and that the crisis has led to the Zairisation[4] of Zimbabwe. Again, let us look at each proposition in turn.

By the end of the 1990s, disaffection had produced strong opposition within civil society and a new political party, the MDC. The linking of urban labour structures with workers on white commercial farms laid the basis for the emergence of a powerful and well-balanced opposition which posed a serious threat to ZANU-PF dominance. In this view, the defeat of the government by these forces in February 2000 in a referendum over a proposed constitutional reform precipitated an attempt to regain lost ground.

The ZANU-PF government is believed to have rigged every subsequent election in a bid to stay in power, violating norms laid down in regional, continental and global agreements specifying internationally accepted criteria for governance and human and political rights. Analysts from this perspective believe that ZANU-PF prefers the total destruction of Zimbabwe to rule by any other party (*Financial Gazette*, 12 July 2007). The concept of impartiality before the law has been abandoned as has the notion of a separation of powers. Key centres of power within the Zimbabwean state, especially the security forces, the judiciary, and major parts of the civil service, are ZANU-PF fiefdoms. The Joint Operations Command continues to act as an unofficial coordinating body for ZANU-PF and allied military interests. The state has been militarised – with retired military figures appointed to key positions and paramilitary forces drawn from 'war veterans' and the youth militia.

Illiberal legislation remains on the books, authorising highly abusive state actions, notably the Public Order and Security Act, the Access to Information and Protection of Privacy Act and the Interception of Communications Act, prohibiting basic freedoms of association, dissent, the press and private communication. The new constitution prevents recourse to the law when land is seized, and police refuse to interfere when land invasions are under way. During and after the course of every election since 2000, ZANU-PF governments have organised a full repertoire of repressive techniques against anyone associated with the MDC – from kidnapping to arson to theft of property to torture to rape and murder. All sectors of civil society – farm workers, peasants, workers, students, the private sector, the church, the judiciary, lawyers, civil society and the opposition – continue to be threatened by these tactics.

In the key area of land, it is held that the reforms should be understood less as the equitable transfer of land from a small class of white commercial farmers to land-poor farmers from the communal areas and more as a tool in the service of a party and a president whose power has rested, to no small degree, on patronage. Proof that the land reform had a largely political agenda can be seen in its timing (it was driven primarily by electoral considerations), its reckless and hasty imposition (without a well-considered and sustainable agricultural strategy), its beneficiaries (the best land has gone to an elite connected to ZANU-PF) and the resulting decline in agricultural production. Even more telling was the fact that the state held vast tracts of land which it had not distributed before it started the land reform. Moreover, the focus on land reform downplayed other key goals central to the liberation struggle – the questions of universal franchise, majority rule and adequate health care, education and employment.

Notably, on economic policy, the opposition to ZANU-PF is divided: one group (including sections of the independent press, key economic advisers to the MDC and the private sector) supports the neoliberal policies which were introduced in Zimbabwe in the early 1990s. In this view, difficulties arose because the government failed to implement the policies fully, and this grouping would return Zimbabwe to the 'economic fundamentals' of this programme. Other MDC supporters, including trade unions and some civil society groups, have opposed neoliberal measures.

All in this camp believe that ZANU-PF has become incompetent, repressive and corrupt. As the formal economy entered its downward spiral, those with access to political power engaged in wholesale looting not only of the white commercial farming sector but also of mineral wealth and state assets. The discovery and development of diamonds in Marange in eastern Zimbabwe rejuvenated this class and provided ZANU-PF with a major source of patronage. In this period, fortunes have been made by a parasitic class located in ZANU-PF, the military and civil service, while the vast majority lead a perilous existence, lacking even the basics.

These, then, are the two principal discourses which compete to explain the dramatic developments in Zimbabwe in the years after 2000. The battle on the intellectual terrain has complemented struggles on the political and material plane. Let us turn now to consider their claims.

Assessing the Zimbabwe debate

In order to assess the merits of the debate sketched above, two separate but related clusters of issues demand attention. The first centres around the role of external factors and especially whether neocolonialism and racism are central in shaping Zimbabwe's crisis. The second cluster assesses the progressive or socialist nature of change in the 2000s in Zimbabwe. It will be argued that a careful examination does not allow an analysis whose logic lies in the past to determine the different terrain of the contemporary period. Although immensely appealing to a region and a continent with bitter memories of colonial rule, a perspective based on the era of the liberation struggle diverts attention from the realities of the class holding state power in Zimbabwe, the nature of its rule, the effect of structural change on its productive base and the future of Zimbabwean development.

Rocky relations with the west

Turning first to the question of anti-imperialism, the Mugabe regime has used nationalism and pan-Africanism to win support from a wide swathe of African public opinion (Phimister and Raftopoulos 2004, 385–400). The reasons for this success are not hard to find. Since the early 1980s, African countries have experienced a harsh policing of economic policy through structural adjustment programmes with mixed to negative results. The return to an overt imperial role by the USA and the UK in the Middle East and Africa helped to fuel strong anti-imperialist sentiment. Mugabe has wasted no opportunity to lay the blame for Zimbabwe's woes on external forces – IFIs and Western countries. In particular, Mugabe and other ZANU-PF leaders focused repeatedly on Britain's historic responsibility for Zimbabwe's catastrophe and also on the damage wrought by international sanctions.

It is argued here that Mugabe's claims misrepresent the recent history of Zimbabwe's relations with Western nations. Although neoliberal macroeconomic policies contributed to the difficulties which followed, the insistence on the central responsibility of the British government for Zimbabwe's crisis is misplaced, and the focus on sanctions is both contrived and erroneous.

Certainly, an unhappy experience with structural adjustment policies set the stage for the tragedy that unfolded and strengthened the conviction that Western powers were determined to effect regime change in Zimbabwe. In the late 1980s and early 1990s, the Zimbabwean Government had hoped to find a way to accelerate growth, to break through foreign exchange constraints, to fund social services and to employ hundreds of thousands of secondary school leavers coming out on to the job market. However, the policies of IFIs failed to deliver significantly in the areas of growth, investment and unemployment, and the trade deficit exploded (Bond 2000, 173–82). Manufacturing output fell by 24% in the 1990s as deindustrialisation ravaged the textile, metals, transport equipment and clothing subsectors (Bond 2000, 176). Foreign debt tripled as a percentage of gross domestic product (GDP) from 8.4% to 21.8% between 1991 and 1996, while inflation averaged about 27% during the Zimbabwe Economic Structural Adjustment Programme (ESAP) period (Bond 2000, 175, 180; Kanyenze 2010).

The deterioration of living standards caused by a sharp reduction in real wages (see Raftopoulos and Phimister 2004, 357) and new cost recovery policies in health, education and other social services, coupled with the growing population of unemployed literate youth, provided fertile grounds for an emergent opposition. Yet, in precisely this period, the IMF insisted that the Zimbabwean Government adopt policies which would heighten class tensions – requiring that price controls on staple foods be abandoned and a tax on luxury imports removed (Bond 2000, 183). For its part, the World Bank promoted the reduction of real wages as a 'brutal but necessary' adjustment to generate export-led growth (Carmody and Taylor 2003).

Not surprisingly, the Mugabe regime became increasingly frustrated by its inability to sustain programmes which it had put in place in the 1980s, especially increases in social sector funding. It became all too obvious that the regime's ability to retain popular support was being damaged when standards of living started to crash. No wonder that many in Zimbabwe see the current crisis as having its origins in policies pushed by IFIs, adopted by the government, and then abandoned. There is no question that these abortive 'reforms' provide part of the structural basis for Zimbabwe's crisis, setting the stage for the Mugabe regime's struggle to stay in power.

While the ZANU-PF government's assessment of the destructive effect of neoliberal policies is understandable, the blame that Mugabe and others have heaped on Britain for Zimbabwe's difficulties has been both excessive and inappropriate. On the central issue of British promises to fund land reform at the Lancaster House Conference preceding independence, the evidence is mixed. Zimbabwean authorities insist, but British

Government representatives deny that Britain agreed to take sole responsibility for funding land reform.

The British position is that its government pledged to contribute to the costs and to rally support from other donors (United Kingdom 2008). Between 1980 and 1985, the UK provided £47 million for land reform and was prepared to do more (*New Zimbabwe*, 18 June 2007). However, the Zimbabwean Government did not respond, and the programme lapsed with £3 million unspent. For about a decade, the issue of funding land reform in Zimbabwe lay dormant. Then in 1997, the British Government returned to the issue in a way that touched a nerve in Zimbabwe. In a clumsy and tactless letter to Zimbabwe's Minister of Agriculture, Claire Short, British Secretary of State for International Development, claimed that the election of a Labour government without links to colonial interests meant Britain no longer had a special responsibility to meet the costs of land purchases in Zimbabwe (Short 1997). For the Zimbabwean Government, this assertion amounted to a betrayal of the solemn promise that had been part of the bargain to secure the Lancaster House agreement preceding independence. British officials further irritated the Zimbabwean Government by insisting that priority should be given to poorer farmers rather than 'cronies' of the government.

In discussions at Commonwealth meetings in Abuja in 2001 after invasions of white farms were well under way, the UK renewed its commitment to provide significant assistance for land reform and promised to bring in other international donors. In turn, the Zimbabwean Government agreed to prevent further occupation of farmlands, to restore the rule of law and to take firm action against intimidation. However, shortly after the meeting, the Zimbabwean Government reneged on its promises, aborting the arrangement with the UK.

Throughout the years that followed, the Mugabe Government singled out Britain and especially Prime Minister Tony Blair and his Labour governments for abuse, arguing against their purported neocolonialism. Even though the British Government continued to provide significant assistance – about $1.25 billion in humanitarian and transitional assistance from 2000 to 2013 (Pocock 2009; DFID 2011) – the imperialist taint meant that it could do little more. While the British handling of Zimbabwean sensitivities was inept and ambiguous, the Zimbabwean emphasis on Britain's role as a significant cause of the crisis is at odds with the historical record.

The use and abuse of 'sanctions'

The Mugabe regime has made similar use of the issue of sanctions against Zimbabwe. As noted earlier, measures were taken by Western countries to prohibit arms sales, forbid travel and freeze the assets of more than 200 members of the Zimbabwean elite and ZANU-PF-aligned companies. The USA also imposed broader economic sanctions linked to IFIs. The targeted sanctions focused on parastatal bodies and senior members of ZANU-PF, the military, the civil service and allied individuals in the private sector. Companies affected by targeted financial sanctions were primarily held in the business wing of ZANU-PF, Zidco Holdings (*The Daily News*, 8 December 2009). These measures were intended to remain in place until Zimbabwe showed signs of progress towards the return of democracy, the rule of law and the completion of the constitutional review process. Recently, the EU has suspended most targeted sanctions. The USA, Australia and Canada retain most measures.

As we have seen, ZANU-PF leaders claim that sanctions are illegal and can be blamed, in large part, for the Zimbabwean crisis and the poverty of Zimbabwean people. The basis for this assertion rests on propaganda and hyperbole. The targeted nature of the sanctions meant that, barring one, they lacked the potential to affect the general population or the larger economy. The only sanctions that might have hurt Zimbabwe's broader economy were provisions that instructed US delegates at multilateral financial institutions to vote against financial aid or debt cancellation for Zimbabwe (Dell 2005). To date, however, there has been no instance when the US delegate has exercised this veto. The decision by the IMF and World Bank to suspend balance of payments and other support was based on the failure of the Zimbabwean Government to service its IFI debts (*Zimbabwe Independent*, 15 November 2013) and differences over economic policy.

Although most Western countries stopped providing bilateral assistance to the Zimbabwean Government in the early 2000s, they continued to offer humanitarian assistance through non-governmental organisations (NGOs), primarily in the form of food aid and help with the HIV/AIDS pandemic. The USA alone provided more than $1.2 billion in aid from 2001 to 2013, and for a time its food aid was feeding one in five Zimbabweans (*Mail & Guardian*, 23 August 2013). Taken together, it is clear that the much-reviled West carried a large number of Zimbabweans throughout the crisis. Moreover, once the Government of National Unity (GNU) became operational in 2009, Western funds poured in. As just one example, the EU and its member states provided more than US$2 billion for assistance to education, water, sanitation, health, agriculture and food aid (*Mail & Guardian*, 11 October 2013).

It is important to remember, moreover, that trade and investment with Europe, the USA and other Western countries were never embargoed although access to foreign lines of credit became difficult given Zimbabwe's notoriety and the stain accompanying sanctions. Nevertheless, throughout the 2000s, trade continued to be substantial and during the GNU trade doubled between Zimbabwe and the EU (*Zimbabwe Independent*, 4 April 2014). Zimbabwe ran sizeable trade surpluses with both the USA and the UK, continued to benefit from the African, Caribbean and Pacific Group of States (ACP)–EU) Partnership Agreement[5] and had status as a Sugar Protocol Country within the Cotonou Framework.[6]

As to foreign direct investment, its dramatic decline for most of the decade reflected an international consensus that Zimbabwe was and is one of the worst places in the world in which to do business. Zimbabwe ranked 170 out of 189 in the World Bank's 2013 report on ease of doing business and 131 out of 148 countries in the 2014 World Economic Forum global competitiveness report, with similar results for most of the period since 2000. The ZANU-PF government's refusal to respect the rule of law or enforce contracts and its policy statements favouring indigenisation over property rights provided a strong disincentive for foreign involvement. Zimbabwe's hyperinflationary period (officially 230 million per cent but unofficially a quintillion) and its plummeting growth rate made Zimbabwe a bad bet for even the most optimistic investor (*Business Day*, 22 August 2008). Once Zimbabwe's currency was dollarised in early 2009, foreign direct investment started to return though cautiously given the uncertainty posed by the indigenisation programme. Although limited by debt arrears (then $7 billion), the Zimbabwean Government was also able to borrow $1.2 billion offshore in the period from 2010 to 2012 (Hawkins 2012). Following ZANU-PF's return to power in 2013 and its initial recommitment to the policy of indigenisation, however, foreign direct investment plummeted.

In any case, despite ZANU-PF's contention to the contrary, neither decisions about investing nor about financial assistance can be construed as 'illegal'. Sovereign states, international bodies and corporations have the right to make such decisions. The drying up of foreign credit for Zimbabwe was a direct consequence of the nature and policies of ZANU-PF governments. It is striking that the call by ZANU-PF leaders for sanctions to be lifted, which would imply a desire for closer economic ties with the West, coexists uneasily with their contention that Western imperialism is the source of Zimbabwe's problems.

Racism and opposition in Zimbabwe

Linked to ZANU-PF charges of Western 'imperialism' has been the assertion that opposition to change in Zimbabwe is a product of racist attitudes. Certainly, there can be no doubt that the plight of white farmers in Zimbabwe attracted international attention and strong reactions from the Western press and Western governments while human rights abuses elsewhere in Africa went unremarked. The West was virtually silent during the war in the Democratic Republic of the Congo (DRC) which killed 3–5 million people and displaced many more. To say the least the Western response to genocide in Rwanda, Darfur and the Central African Republic and to continued suffering in the eastern DRC and the Sudans has been lame and ineffectual.

At the same time, the Zimbabwean Government itself has operated on an explicitly racial basis in its project of dispossessing white farmers. No one put the matter more succinctly than Joice Mujuru, vice-president of Zimbabwe. 'They (white farmers) call themselves Zimbabweans', she said. 'They are not. I am a Zimbabwean. When will you learn? Africa is for black Africans' (Freeth 2012).

Although the government claimed that it was reappropriating land taken from Africans during the colonial period, almost all of the large-scale commercial farmers whose land was seized were not descendants of original colonial settlers. Fully 80% of farmers had not inherited farms, and only 5% came from pioneer stock (Selby 2004). In addition, between 70% and 82% of commercial farm deeds had changed hands after independence, following assurances from the ZANU-PF government that it had no interest in them (Selby 2004; Karimakwenda 2006). As Dale Dore observed:

> the vast majority of white farmers had therefore, like a growing number of their black compatriots, paid the full market value for their farms, including land, and were granted full legal title to it. They did not steal land from anyone. (2013, 2)

Moreover, under the 1985 Land Acquisition Act, land could not be purchased without government permission. By allowing sales to go through, the government signalled that it did not have an interest in the land that was being sold. In 1992, amendments introduced a Certificate of No Present Interest, which strengthened the government position, allowing the purchase of previously offered land when funds came available. However, these provisions became moot once the fast-track land reform began in earnest, after which (with some few exceptions) land policy was designed to eliminate whites from farming in Zimbabwe. Hence, the argument that white farmers did not deserve compensation for 'stolen property' not only repudiated the government's prior assurances but also rewrote its own rules (Shaw 2003, 75–89).

Justifying the expropriations by referring to the history of occupation and settler colonialism also tended to skip over the history of land reform in the period since independence. For most of the first two decades especially after 1984, the government did not seem to be interested in a serious programme of land reform and actively discouraged land occupations by squatters (Moyo 2004, 8–11). As noted above, the government let a British programme of assistance for land reform lapse with a balance of funds unspent. From 1997 on, the issue returned to the forefront when war veterans began to agitate for a more radical land reform in the light of glaring inequities. However, it was the government's defeat in the constitutional referendum in 2000 and the growing power of the MDC which prompted the major assault on the white commercial farming sector. Mugabe made no secret of his feeling that in supporting the MDC the white community had betrayed and abandoned him. The deep-seated resentment within Zimbabwe about the continuing racial imbalance in landownership provided him with the tinder to move against this group. Hence, the government's decision to jettison its alliance with white agricultural capital was provoked as much or more by contemporary political reasons as it was by genuine issues of injustice and historical dispossession.[7]

In 2007/2008, the ZANU-PF government turned to other sectors of the economy when it passed the Indigenisation and Economic Empowerment Bill which stipulated that all foreign-owned companies would be required to transfer 51% of their businesses to indigenous Zimbabweans – defined as a person who was disadvantaged by 'unfair discrimination on the grounds of his or her race' before the country's independence in 1980. Since 2010, ZANU-PF ministers have spearheaded a drive to force foreign-owned mining companies and banks to comply with the programme and have promised to extend these provisions to all other sectors of the economy.

A crucially important second dimension of framing the reforms in terms of an anti-white discourse was that it attempted to mask the bitter power struggle within Zimbabwe's black population. Black opposition to the ZANU-PF regime stung the ZANU-PF government far more than the purported racist prejudice of a tiny white minority (some estimate fewer than 30,000 out of a total population of 12–13 million). The membership of the MDC and of trade unions, church and NGO coalitions within civil society is almost entirely black as is the independent press.

Moreover, while the beneficiaries of the land reform are black, the overwhelming majority of victims of the land reform have also been black. These include the 30,000–35,000 small black settlers pushed off farms by well-connected elites, the 350,000 farm workers and their families (a total of 1.8 million people) and the 250,000 seasonal and casual worker families, of whom about 2/3 to 3/4 were left jobless, homeless and destitute (Research and Advocacy Unit and Justice for Agriculture Trust 2009, 2; Neill 2004, 15, 35; Hartnack 2005, 173–192; Scoones 2008, 3). It has been conservatively estimated that 1% of the farm worker population died (about 10,000 people; Zimbabwe Human Rights NGO Forum and the Justice for Agriculture Trust in Zimbabwe 2007, 2–3).[8]

Thus, the portrayal of land reform in racial terms obscures more than it reveals. Although attention has focused disproportionately on the ZANU-PF government's abuse of white farmers, there is no question that Zimbabwe's black population has suffered far more from government ill treatment in the 2000s.

The progressive or socialist nature of transformation in Zimbabwe

The portrayal of the Zimbabwean crisis in terms of racism, neocolonialism and imperialism has also tended to distract attention from crucial dimensions of power inside Zimbabwe itself. Growing class divisions and inequalities have accompanied the brutality and corruption of a highly repressive state. The undoubted power and influence of Zimbabwean security forces also opens to question the 'progressive' nature of the class in power. Neither Zimbabwe's military nor its political class is known for their pro-poor sympathies. These factors help in an assessment of the claim (as some on the Left would have it) that the approach taken by the ZANU-PF government before the GNU was 'progressive' or 'socialist' and that its goal was revolutionary transformation (Moyo and Yeros 2007, 106; Mamdani 2008).

On this point, the work of John Saul remains prescient. In an early and controversial article, Saul emphasised the ways in which 'petty-bourgeois politicking' –the jockeying for position based on factionalism, personality and the instrumentalism of ethnic issues – had forestalled the deepening of the revolutionary project of Zimbabwean liberation movements (Saul 1979). At the time of Zimbabwean independence, he wrote cautiously of Mugabe 'cast ... in the role of Sphinx, guarding his options and seeming deliberately to muddy the ideological waters' (Saul 1980, 38). Indeed, Saul warned the Left against 'waiting for Mugabe'. When he assessed the prospects of Zimbabwe moving beyond 'primitive' or bourgeois nationalism to a more revolutionary nationalism (defined as realising the interests of the people as a whole rather than the interests of a small group), he noted that 'considerable controversy swirls around the question ... of just what kind of promise of continued forward movement ZANU has to offer' (Saul 1980, 34).

In the current period of crisis in Zimbabwe, one finds a deepening of the pathology foreshadowed by this analysis – the intense petty-bourgeois politicking as rivals battle to succeed Mugabe, the evaporation of the revolutionary promise of ZANU-PF, and Mugabe, still the Sphinx, confusing his would-be successors as he struggles to hang on to power indefinitely. Indeed, the structures of power which have emerged within the Zimbabwean state have been shaped to meet the exclusive interests of Mugabe, ZANU-PF and military leaders. National security forces (police and military) have been pressed into direct service, and state institutions have been militarised and transformed into partisan bodies. Carte blanche has been given to paramilitary forces (the youth militia and 'war veterans'), and ZANU-PF members continue to act as a law unto themselves.

This configuration has enabled a high level of abuse of human, civil and political rights which is more characteristic of a quasi-fascist than a socialist state (Scarnecchia 2006). During the 2000s, Zimbabwean security forces embarked on a series of commandist 'Operations' –Murambatsvina, Maguta, Chikorokoza Chapera/Isitsheketsha Sesiphelile, Mavhotera Papi and others – which led to successive waves of dispossession. Farm workers pushed off commercial farms, small farmers losing their properties, vendors in the informal sector having their goods stolen and their stalls destroyed, residents in backyard shacks of high density areas having their homes smashed, small miners expelled from active mining and farming communities losing their ancestral lands to mining companies; all these dispossessions have added trauma to impoverishment.

While some writers on the Left have downplayed civil and political rights as liberal bourgeois concepts which do not come to grips with material inequality (Yeros 2002; Moyo and Yeros 2005), the violation of these rights has not led to a more egalitarian society either. The blatant enrichment of a tiny urban elite and their clients sits uneasily with the socialist claim, especially in a situation of widespread poverty and unemployment (estimated at about 85%). According to government statistics (Zimstat), most of Zimbabwe's estimated population of 12–13 million can be classified as poor, while 16% live in extreme poverty (*Zimbabwe Independent*, 19 July 2013). At one point in the mid-2000s, life expectancy had collapsed to 37 years for men and 34 years for women.

The class that emerged at the top of the ZANU-PF state has been prone to conspicuous consumption, but it has yet to demonstrate that it can seriously engage in economic development. A parasitic accumulation model (asset stripping) has been the norm rather than one featuring technological and productive transformation. In the period of hyperinflation, vast profits were gained from arbitrage (as a rapacious elite obtained foreign exchange, grain, fuel and agricultural inputs at subsidised rates and sold these goods on the black market) and rent seeking (economic opportunities made available only to cronies of the government). The looting of Zimbabwe's mineral wealth – gold, platinum and the diamond fields of Marange – followed on. The 2014 'Salarygate' revelations of remuneration for heads of parastatals [with the standout being Cuthbert ('Cashbert') Dube as head of the non-profit Premier Service Medical Aid Society bringing home $6.4 million annually] repeated this general pattern.

By contrast, labour in both rural and urban areas has become more vulnerable than at any time since independence. By 2012, only 700,000 people were employed in the formal economy (excluding agriculture and private domestic service), or 14% of the workforce (Hawkins 2012). Those who are employed in the civil service receive paltry monthly salaries (about half the amount needed to live a normal life); even so, in 2013, they consumed 75% of government income (*New Zimbabwe*, 13 May 2014).

Recent research has shown that between 2000 and 2010, 224,000 jobs were lost on large commercial farms while 287,00 jobs were created on resettled farms – a net gain but qualified by the 1.5 million growth in Zimbabwe's population (Hawkins 2013). In the early years of the land reform, wages and working conditions for agricultural workers on black-owned farms were worse than in the days of white commercial agriculture, as were employer–employee relations (Sachikonye 2003, 46; Moyo 2004, 34). Most farm workers became casual rather than full-time workers and were paid on the basis of piecework (Neill 2004, 34). As a matter of deliberate policy, few farm workers (about 5%) were granted land (Moyo 2011, 946). When inflation exploded, farm workers (who received at best about 4% of the basic amount needed for a low-income consumer basket) fled the agricultural sector in droves (*Zimbabwe Independent*, 19 January 2007).

On the central question of whether land reform has made landownership more egalitarian, the evidence is mixed. In central ways, the reform has served the principle of redistributive justice and transformed the prospects of thousands of farmers. All but a few hundred of the original 4500 white farmers have been pushed off their farms, and the old dualistic structure of agriculture has been dismantled, opening up possibilities for a more diversified agrarian system.

In the scheme for small farmers (the A-1 land reform) which constituted 66% of the total land redistributed (Government of Zimbabwe 2003, 5), 245,000 farming families gained land (Hanlon, Manjengwa, and Smart 2013). Of these, 87% of the beneficiaries were the rural poor (including communal area farmers) and the urban poor (Moyo 2004, 26–27). A further 20,000 black farmers have received land under the A-2 part of the land reform – the scheme for medium- and large-scale commercial farmers (Moyo 2011, 945).

Although government land audits have not been released, reports indicate that a considerable proportion of prime commercial agricultural land has been allocated to allies of the ruling elite. The Zimbabwean press is replete with stories of multiple farm ownership by prominent politicians, judges, bureaucrats, and army, air force and police officers. Many have little agricultural experience and have let great estates lie fallow once the initial crops have been harvested or have asset stripped and moved on. Some are leasing the farms back to their original owners in what is left of the white farming community. Meanwhile, the vast majority of Zimbabweans (at least 75%) still live in rural areas with inadequate land on which to farm; there has been little decongestion of communal lands (about 10%; Moyo 2004, 30).

Also, although the coalition government attempted to provide inputs and assistance for small farmers, their absence for much of the decade meant that in many parts of the countryside the reform initiative was stillborn (Scoones 2008, 3–4; Kinsey 2009, 15–16). Government policy not to grant title deeds for new farmers means that tenure is insecure and bank credit is not forthcoming. In many cases, growers are channelled into contract farming, with foreign companies acting as their source of inputs and credit.

Despite these difficulties, in some areas, notably Masvingo province and parts of Mashonaland, there is evidence that 'where there is low capital investment and a reliance on local labour, settlers have done reasonably well, particularly in the wetter parts of the province' (Scoones 2008, 1; Kinsey 2009, 6–7). The hope is that recent improvements in tobacco and maize production are signs of a turnaround and that the success celebrated by Ian Scoones, Joseph Hanlon and their co-authors will be replicated more broadly (Scoones et al. 2010; Hanlon, Manjengwa, and Smart 2013). Generally, the reform has produced a wider range of farmers cultivating more land for food and exports than was the case before 2000 (Moyo 2011, 961). Without question, the social base of the economy has been broadened.

At the same time, the overall record is bleak: total agricultural production has declined precipitously – by about 50% between 2000 and 2012 (Hawkins 2012). Agricultural value added in constant 2000 prices in 2010 was lower than at independence in 1980 and less than half its peak in 2001; output per worker in agriculture rose by a third between 1980 and 2001, but by 2010 had fallen 56% (Hawkins 2013). By 2007, losses to the commercial farming sector after expropriation were estimated to amount to a staggering US$8.4 billion (Zimbabwe Human Rights NGO Forum and the Justice for Agriculture Trust in Zimbabwe 2007, 2). As commercial agriculture had formerly provided a third of the country's GDP, the land invasions dramatically cut the state's tax revenues, a reality which ultimately led the government to print money.

Close linkages between agriculture and industry meant that once the large-scale farms were eliminated, agro-industry closed down as well. Manufacturing output (by volume) was lower in 2012 than in 1980 and two-thirds below its peak (Hawkins 2013). Zimbabwe's real GDP fell 40%, from $6.6 billion in 2000 to $4.1 billion in 2010, and real per capita incomes were 37% lower in 2011 than they were at independence in April 1980 (Hawkins 2012; Kinsey 2009, 20). Little wonder that between one-quarter and one-third of the population of Zimbabwe has emigrated to other countries in an effort to survive and to support families at home.

The structural shift in agriculture also opens to question the issue of Zimbabwe's overall development trajectory. One of the most sophisticated commercial agricultural sectors in the world has been destroyed and its technological lead abandoned with only the promise here and there of a transformed alternative. The future for an agricultural sector based on small-scale producers is, at best, uncertain, especially where new farmers face competition in regional and global markets from highly productive and efficient firms. For the domestic economy, the task ahead is to rebuild value chains between myriad small farms and agro-industry in order to revive the industrial sector as well. If these connections are not made, then the programme of land resettlement may have driven the Zimbabwean economy on to a narrower path based on the exploitation of minerals accompanied by continued deindustrialisation (Hawkins 2013).

The question, then, of whether the 'revolution' in Zimbabwe's productive base amounts to a movement forward to a more progressive future is highly problematic. Excluding the brief upturn during the 2008–2013 coalition government, the record of ZANU-PF governments has been one of economic contraction, deepening inequality, poverty, corruption and harshly repressive politics. The end to the white commercial agricultural sector may have rid Zimbabwe of a powerful minority and a dualistic agricultural structure, but the inevitably slow process of developing a productive alternative has left its economic base weakened and its population impoverished. Only the development of the Marange diamond fields, with annual revenues reported to range between $2 billion to $4 billion (Cross 2011), rescued the Zimbabwean power elite from the crisis for which it bears most of the responsibility. Now that the surface alluvial deposits show signs of exhaustion even this resource may not be sufficient to cushion the state and the elite from the harsh realities which have accompanied its policies.

Indeed, ZANU-PF's return to power in the July 2013 election has been accompanied by a resumption of severe economic crisis. Deindustrialisation has accelerated with 1300 jobs lost in the first quarter of 2014 (*Zimbabwe Independent*, 30 May 2014). The government has been unable to secure adequate financial assistance from IFIs, from the West or even from China. At writing, it has been forced to borrow to finance recurrent expenditures, unable even to pay civil servant salaries fully and on time. Foreign investors have shied away, dissuaded by the return to strong if confusing signals on indigenisation. Most Zimbabweans again rely on remittances from the diaspora.

The country continues to be ruled by Robert Mugabe who at 90 is reported by WikiLeaks to suffer from terminal metastasized cancer and the inevitable vagaries of old age. His determination to remain president until his death is heightened not only by his fear of being held to account at the International Criminal Court but also by the prospect of his party disintegrating in succession battles. Allied to this project is a shadow state consisting not only of core political and military hardliners but also business and criminal elements in Zimbabwe linked to their equivalents in the region and in the Middle East and Asia. Zimbabwe's great mineral wealth and especially its diamond boom in the last few years have reinvigorated these networks of power, making the prospect of significant change in the near future problematic. The implosion of the MDC following its electoral defeat in 2013 has removed, for the time being, any significant organised opposition to the ZANU-PF government.

Conclusion: Quo Vadis Zimbabwe

In conclusion, the interpretation of the crisis by ZANU-PF, its supporters and intellectual fellow travellers continues to hold a formidable power over events. The symbolic ejection of white farmers tapped into strong feelings about African dispossession and mistreatment by the West. The potency of the attack on Western imperialism and neocolonialism, the argument that African resources (especially land) belong to black Africans and the visceral opposition to sanctions have had broad appeal in Africa and among sections of the intelligentsia. Taken together with the material bases of power (especially access to Zimbabwe's mineral wealth), this ideological force helped ZANU-PF win the day in the 2013 election. Against this view, a careful look at the nature of the regime in power through most of Zimbabwe's post-independence history casts a different light on questions of race, class and, above all, the progressive quality (or not) of Zimbabwe's 'revolution'.

This article has argued that questions of Western malign intent have diverted attention from the dynamics of power inside Zimbabwe which have produced a pathological polity and massive economic deterioration. It is argued here that the abandonment of basic rights has not been accompanied by an improvement in the well-being of ordinary Zimbabweans; their position is worse in many instances than it was at independence. As to the revolutionary promise of the transformation under way in Zimbabwe, prospects are limited in the economic sphere – with a focus on enclave mineral development and an as yet embryonic sector of small-scale agriculture. In the political sphere, the state continues to accommodate an ossified brutal elite, which monopolises power and the nation's resources – an eerie echo of the settler colonial state it replaced at independence.

Notes

1. A very early version of this article was published in *Historia* 50, no. 2 (2005), 287–310.
2. Other authors who subscribe to this position (Mamdani, Moyo and Yeros) have not endorsed ZANU-PF's propositions about political participation and citizenship. They did argue, however, that the opposing camp paid disproportionate attention to 'liberal bourgeois' questions of human and civil rights and neglected economic and social rights.
3. To be called 'totemless' is an insult, meaning one has no father to look up to for guidance and no genealogy. On a trip to Rome in June 2002, Mugabe told Zimbabweans there: *Ndiko kune mitupo kumaruwa. Mitupo iri muBulawayo ndeipi? Mitupo irimuHarare ndeipi?* [What totems exist in Harare and Bulawayo? Totems are only found in rural areas.] Cited in 'Editor's Memo', *Zimbabwe Independent*, 2002.
4. Zairisation refers to the state policy of Zaire (now the Democratic Republic of the Congo) nationalising large foreign-owned export-oriented firms and placing political cronies in charge of them. The new managers mismanaged the firms and drained them of their assets but remained politically loyal to Mobutu, then president.
5. The ACP–EU Economic Partnership Agreement is a trade deal between the EU and former European colonies in Africa, the Caribbean and the Pacific region that offers favourable access to the EU market.
6. The Sugar Protocol permits certain ACP countries to export a fixed quantity of sugar to the EU annually at a preferential price.
7. As a sideline, it is interesting to note that public opinion surveys found that the overwhelming majority (76%) of respondents held that the government should abide by the law and pay the owners compensation for their land and property (Chikwanha, Sithole, and Bratton 2004, 12).
8. Farm workers bore the full brunt of the attacks which accompanied farm invasions, many of them left destitute on rural roads deprived of food, shelter, health care and other forms of

support. The survivors migrated to squatter settlements in peri-urban areas where they faced another round of dispossession in Operation Murambatsvina, became artisanal miners facing further state persecution or migrated to work on South African farms.

References

Bond, Patrick. 2000. "Zimbabwe's Economic Crisis." *Labour, Capital and Society* 33 (2): 162–191.

Bond, Patrick, and Masimba Manyanya. 2002. *Zimbabwe's Plunge – Exhausted Nationalism, Neoliberalism and the Search for Social Justice.* Trenton, NJ: Africa World Press.

Carmody, Pádraig, and Scott Taylor. 2003. "Industry and the Urban Sector in Zimbabwe's Political Economy." *African Studies Quarterly* 7 (2): 53–80.

Chikwanha, Annie, Tulani Sithole, and Michael Bratton. 2004. "The Power of Propaganda: Public Opinion in Zimbabwe, 2004." AfroBarometer Working Paper No. 42. Cape Town: Institute for Democracy in South Africa.

Concerned Africa Scholars. 2009. *Bulletin 82.* http://concernedafricascholars.org/bulletin/issue82/.

Cross, Eddie. 2011. "Presentation to Parliament on the State of Diamond Extractions at Marange and in Support of a Motion on the Subject Submitted for Debate to the Zimbabwe House of Assembly." House of Assembly of Zimbabwe. 27 October.

Dell, Christopher. 2005. "Plain Talk about the Zimbabwean Economy." Speech presented by the U.S. Ambassador to Zimbabwe at Africa University, Mutare, Zimbabwe, November 2.

Department for International Development (DFID). 2011. *Annual Report and Accounts 2010–11.* London: The Stationery Office. https://www.gov.uk/government/uploads/system/uploads/attachment_data/file/67477/Annual-report-2011-vol1.pdf.

Dore, Dale. 2013. "Remaking History: Citizenship, Power, and the Recasting of Heroes and Villains." *Sokwanele,* October 2.

Elich, Gregory. 2005. "What the West Doesn't Want to Know – Zimbabwe's Fight for Justice." *Counterpunch,* Weekend Edition, May 7–9. http://www.counterpunch.org/.

Freeth, Ben. 2012. "Racial Discrimination in Zimbabwe: A Systematic Program of Abuse – Part 4." *Nehanda Radio,* December 11.

Government of Zimbabwe. 2003. *Report of the Presidential Land Review Committee on the Implementation of the Fast Track Land Reform Programme, 2000–2002* ('The Utete Report').

Hanlon, Joseph, Jeanette Manjengwa, and Teresa Smart. 2013. *Zimbabwe Takes Back Its Land.* Sterling, VA: Kumarian Press.

Hartnack, Andrew. 2005. "'My Life Got Lost': Farm Workers and Displacement in Zimbabwe." *Journal of Contemporary African Studies* 23 (2): 173–192. doi:10.1080/02589000500176032.

Hawkins, Tony. 2012. "Counting the Cost of Zimbabwean Land Reform." *Politicsweb,* November 1.

Hawkins, Tony. 2013. "Inconvenient Truths about Land Reform in Zimbabwe." *Nehanda Radio,* June 5.

Kanyenze, Godfrey. 2010. "Development Deferred." Notes, November 6.

Karimakwenda, Tererai. 2006. "JAG Says Compensation of White Farmers a Scam." *SW Radio Africa,* June 12.

Kinsey, Bill H. 2009. "Multiple Realities: An Assessment of the Impact of a Generation of Land Redistribution on Food Security and Livelihoods in Zimbabwe." Paper presented at the Annual Meeting of the African Studies Association, New Orleans, LA, November 19–22.

Mamdani, Mahmood. 2008. "Lessons of Zimbabwe." *London Review of Books* 30 (23): 17–21.

Moore, David. 2004. "Marxism and Marxist Intellectuals in Schizophrenic Zimbabwe: How Many Rights for Zimbabwe's Left? A Comment." *Historical Materialism* 12 (4): 405–425. doi:10.1163/1569206043505257.

Moyo, Sam. 2004. "The Land and Agrarian Question in Africa: the Case of Zimbabwe." Draft Paper, University of Fort Hare, September 25.

Moyo, Sam. 2011. "Changing Agrarian Relations after Redistributive Land Reform in Zimbabwe. *Journal of Peasant Studies* 38 (5): 939–966. doi:10.1080/03066150.2011.634971.

Moyo, Sam, and Paris Yeros. 2005. "Land Occupations and Land Reform in Zimbabwe: Towards the National Democratic Revolution." In *Reclaiming the Land*, edited by Sam Moyo and Paris Yeros, 165–205. London: Zed Press.

Moyo, Sam, and Paris Yeros. 2007. "The Radicalised State: Zimbabwe's Interrupted Revolution." *Review of African Political Economy* 34 (111): 103–121. doi:10.1080/03056240701340431.

Ncube, Pius, Roger Bate, and Richard Tren. 2005. "State in Fear: Zimbabwe's Tragedy is Africa's Shame." *Africa Fighting Malaria*, July 6.

Neill, Timothy. 2004. "Labour and Union Issues in the Zimbabwean Agricultural Sector in 2004." MA thesis, University of KwaZulu-Natal.

Phimister, Ian, and Brian Raftopoulos. 2004. "Mugabe, Mbeki and the Politics of Anti-imperialism." *Review of African Political Economy* 31 (101): 385–400. doi:10.1080/0305624042000295503.

Pocock, Andrew. 2009. "British Ambassador to Zimbabwe, Interview with Violet Gonda." *Hot Seat*, Short Wave Radio Africa, June 26.

Raftopoulos, Brian. 2005. "Nation, Race and History in Zimbabwean Politics." In *Zimbabwe: Injustice and Political Reconciliation*, edited by Brian Raftopoulos and Tyrone Savage, 160–175. Cape Town: Institute for Justice and Reconciliation.

Raftopoulos, Brian. 2006. "The Zimbabwe Crisis and the Challenges for the Left." *Journal of Southern African Studies* 32 (2): 203–219. doi:10.1080/03057070600655988.

Raftopoulos, Brian, and Ian Phimister. 2004. "Zimbabwe Now: The Political Economy of Crisis and Coercion." *Historical Materialism* 12 (4): 355–382. doi:10.1163/1569206043505301.

Research and Advocacy Unit and Justice for Agriculture Trust. 2009. *If Something Is Wrong... The Invisible Suffering of Commercial Farm Workers and Their Families Due to 'Land Reform.'* Report produced for the General Agricultural and Plantation Workers Union of Zimbabwe, November 11.

Sachikonye, Lloyd M. 2003. "The Situation of Commercial Farm Workers after Land Reform in Zimbabwe." A report prepared for the Farm Community Trust of Zimbabwe, March. http://www.sarpn.org/documents/d0000359/P343_Sachikonye.pdf.

Saul, John S. 1979. "Transforming the Struggle in Zimbabwe." In *The State and Revolution in Eastern Africa*, edited by John S. Saul, 107–122. New York: Monthly Review Press.

Saul, John S. 1980. "Zimbabwe: The Next Round." *Monthly Review* 32 (4): 38. doi:10.14452/MR-032-04-1980-08_1.

Scarnecchia, Timothy. 2006. "The 'Fascist Cycle' in Zimbabwe 2000–2005." *Journal of Southern African Studies* 32 (2): 221–237. doi:10.1080/03057070600656085.

Schwab, Klaus, ed. 2013. *The Global Competitiveness Report 2013–2014*. Geneva: World Economic Forum.

Scoones, Ian. 2008. "A New Start for Zimbabwe?" Unpublished paper, Institute of Development Studies. http://www.ids.ac.uk/index.cfm?objectid=0FA6E4C8-B4D1-C973-CE2EBDA191066187.

Scoones, Ian, Nelson Marongwe, Blasio Mavedzenge, Jacob Mahenehene, Felix Murimbarimba, and Chrispen Sukume. 2010. *Zimbabwe's Land Reform – Myths and Realities*. Oxford: James Currey Press.

Selby, Angus. 2004. *Private Communication*. November 1.

Shaw, William H. 2003. "'They Stole Our Land': Debating the Expropriation of White Farms in Zimbabwe." *Journal of Modern African Studies* 41 (1): 75–89. doi:10.1017/S0022278X02004159.

Short, Claire. 1997. "Letter from the Hon Claire Short, Secretary of State for International Development to Hon Kumbirai Kangai MP, Minister of Agriculture and Land." November 5.

Yeros, Paris. 2002. "Zimbabwe and the Dilemmas of the Left." *Historical Materialism* 10 (2): 3–15. doi:10.1163/156920602320318066.

Zimbabwe Human Rights NGO Forum and the Justice for Agriculture Trust in Zimbabwe. 2007. *Adding Insult to Injury – A Preliminary Report on Human Rights Violations on Commercial Farms, 2000 to 2005*. June.

Land resistance in Zambia: a case study of the Luana Farmers' Cooperative

Grace-Edward Galabuzi

Department of Politics and Public Administration, Ryerson University, Toronto, Canada

This article focuses on local struggles and new social practices in Zambia, a country rarely discussed when investigating sites of resistance in the region. It reviews the economic history of Zambia, highlighting the centrality of mining to the country's political economy and the effects of the privatisation of Zambia's copper mines, one central part of the broader liberalisation programme undertaken in the 1990s, on former miners and mining communities. Spontaneous opposition to resettlement of local communities, as required by new private mine and landowners, led resistance to take on a more organised form, notably in the formation of the Luana Farmers' Cooperative. The cooperative met with some success under very challenging economic and political conditions, which may fall far short of a fundamental repudiation of neoliberal restructuring, but nonetheless strengthened the survival capacities and political clout of some of those most harshly affected by it.

In the 1990s, the Zambian economy embarked on a liberalisation programme that culminated in the privatisation of Zambia's copper mines and other state assets. The programme had the effect of unsettling pre-existing social relations, in the process of creating new winners and losers. This article uses the Luana Farmers' Cooperative as a case study to demonstrate how resistance to capitalist restructuring can generate new forms of social and economic practices, discourses and identities in post-independence Southern African states such as Zambia. This article explains that the rationalisation of Zambia's copper production activities displaced thousands of workers who were forced to eke out a living through subsistence agricultural activities. For a time, the government permitted workers to access state lands for that purpose. However, the ambitions of the Zambian elite, who embraced globalisation and sought ways to engage in export-oriented agriculture for the global market, required large tracts of land. This land was amassed in part through the privatisation of the lands the ex-miner subsistence farmers had been cultivating. This put the two into conflict, drawing in the state, which initially sided with the elites and sought to appropriate the squatter farms. The Luana farmers were forced to take defensive action by mobilising to confront both the state and the elites – ultimately they were able to secure their right to subsistence through farming, at least partially and for the short term. The question remains whether they will be able to parlay that success into longer term and more systemic transformation of the Zambian economy.

Engagements such as those led by the Luana Farmers' Cooperative emerge on the margins of a globalising capitalist order, resisting both the effects of economic restructuring on their livelihoods and the new role of the state, which represents global and domestic business interests rather than a broader 'national interest' as was the case during and immediately after independence (Moyo 2002). What are we to make of movements such as the Luana farmers? Are they simply defensive, or do they carry with them practices, discourses and identities of resistance that could serve as the basis for a broadly based, multi-locational and potentially pan-Southern African counter-hegemonic movement? I argue here that these practices, incubated in local, marginal places, present the seeds of counter-hegemonic practices that can be disseminated, modelled or simply replicated in other spaces, allowing for the emergence of particular modes of resistance to inform broader anti-capitalist struggles. Whether they can do so remains an open question, and one that will be determined by the organising capacity of the locally based movements themselves. However, this case study does show that the redefinition of the nation as a space has disarticulated authority from the state towards global market regulation and donor-driven governance while dialectically producing locally situated, marginal but radical movements that opportunistically challenge capitalist logic in order to sustain everyday life. These movements, in effect, privilege local space as the most effective site of resistance against the forces of globalising neoliberalism. Only at the local level do autonomy, social control, popular democracy and environmental sustainability present an alternative conceptualisation that is antithetical to the logic of a globalising capitalism. Yet at the same time, in the Zambian case at least, this form of resistance appears to presage a new form of national politics, based on a renewed set of demands on the state to meet the immediate material needs of the majority and to represent their interests against domestic and international elites.

Background: copper mining in Zambia

Zambia became an independent state with great promise in 1964 due to its mineral riches, predominantly copper, and a *per capita* income higher than Kenya, Egypt, Brazil, Malaysia, South Korea and Turkey (Ferguson 1999, 5–6). Urbanisation, waged employment and industrialisation maintained their pace after independence, with the transformation most visible in the capital city and the copper-producing areas, referred to as the Copperbelt. At its peak, the mining workforce was 62,000 people (Kaunda 2002), and many more people relied on the cash wages and infrastructure of the Copperbelt for further economic opportunities. Due in large part to the country's continued reliance on copper, the Zambian economy has been in decline since the mid-1970s, as copper production capacity fell from 670,000 tonnes in 1979 to 325,000 tonnes by 1999 (Ferguson 1999, 7). Falling world demand for copper through most of the past four decades and sharply declining terms of trade had a dramatic effect on the quantity of copper mined and thus on the country's economy (Ferguson 1999, 7). Despite the decline in world copper prices and the volume mined, copper continued to account for between 80% and 90% of Zambia's foreign earnings and 10% of gross domestic production until recently (Hansungule, Feeney, and Palmer 1998), making copper production the linchpin of the country's industrial sector and the economic lifeblood of the Copperbelt region.

Thus, the decline of the copper economy in Zambia in the late twentieth century can be viewed as a crisis of modernity (Ferguson 1999).

The decline in copper prices and production, coupled with rising oil prices and interest rates, triggered a debt crisis that drove Zambia to international financial institutions like the International Monetary Fund (IMF) and the World Bank in the late 1970s. In return, these donors were accorded a significant and growing role in shaping the country's socio-economic policy (Wulf 1988). At the behest of the IMF, the government implemented widespread economic policy changes beginning in 1983. Typical of structural adjustment programmes implemented elsewhere in Africa, the government devalued the currency and implemented cuts in social spending. Further austerity measures were introduced in the mid-1980s. These included the removal of subsidies on the staple food, mealie meal, in 1986 and a steep rise in the price of fuel in 1987. The IMF and World Bank's policy influence continued even during Zambia's highly public split from the IMF in 1987, which was sparked by domestic protests against rising food prices following the removal of subsidies. At that time, Zambia unilaterally limited debt payments and rescinded food price and exchange rate liberalisation. The combination of debt payment limitation, disqualification from debt relief due to its rogue status with the IMF, and continuing stagnation in export earnings meant the country's debt continued to mount. By 1995, debt servicing took 41 cents of every export dollar, and total debt was approximately $650 per person, more than 40% higher than per capital gross domestic product (Ferguson 1999, 7–8).

In 1991, Zambia held multi-party elections for the first time since Kenneth Kaunda's one-party regime came to power at independence in 1964 under the United National Independence Party (UNIP). UNIP embodied the post-colonial conceptions of modernity, industrialisation, urbanisation and the obligations of citizenship that characterised Zambia's early development model, which incorporated the notion of social protection analogous to the welfare state regimes in the global North. Kaunda called his vision 'humanism', describing it as an African form of socialism based on a hybrid of traditional notions of collective social protection and an embrace of modernity. The initial post-colonial period unfolded under an internationalist regime that expected extensive state involvement in building domestic economies and fostering industrialisation. UNIP used this domestic consensus and enabling international environment to impose a one-party state that would eventually become so insular that it fell victim of popular protest, which led to the downfall of the party and the state-led model of development it represented.

The Movement for Multiparty Democracy (MMD) was elected under the promise of championing liberal political rights along with economic reforms that would pull the country from its economic crisis. However, it did not take long for the tensions inherent in the MMD programme of political reform, which aimed at unleashing popular democratic participation while simultaneously entrenching private property rights and market regulation, to come to the fore. The privatisation process empowered certain social groups and disempowered others, privileged certain government departments and disadvantaged others, and opened the way for foreign aid donors to have disproportionate influence on policy development. The process also created new alliances that facilitated the shift in mining and related policy away from the state-led focus on national regulation of production and consumption, which favoured national economic considerations, towards a commitment to global flexibility and competitiveness. Such an approach converged with other mining regimes to foster a competitive environment with regard to foreign direct investment and a global 'least cost production' model as the primary consideration for corporate investment decisions. One consequence was that the state-owned mining company, Zambia Consolidated Copper Mines (ZCCM), was broken up into nine properties and sold to several transnational mining companies. Anglo-American, which had developed and owned many of Zambia's mines in the colonial era, acquired the largest of the privatised mine assets. The government, international donors and corporate leaders all expressed optimism that Zambia would enjoy prosperity once again as a result of the privatisation. This promise did not come to fruition, however, and underlying problems in the industry led Anglo-American to sell its Copperbelt holdings (Hansungule, Feeney, and Palmer 1998).

The mining policy changes were one component in a broader shift towards a globally oriented, transnational capital-led process of restructuring. Under this vision, decision-making and the adjudication of the claims of key social groups or 'stakeholders' with an interest in the economy shifted to favour the market and especially the most powerful market actors. One effect of these changes was new class formations, with ascendant 'domestic capitalist elites' engaged in new forms of capital accumulation. Simultaneously, an urban working class was displaced and marginalised by the restructuring of the copper industry from public ownership 'in the national interest' to transnational private ownership – many were 'repeasantised' in the sense that they turned to subsistence agricultural production and relied on family labour as an economic survival strategy (Radfield 1956; Moyo and Yeros 2005). Privatisation cost 60% of mineworkers their jobs (Kaunda 2002), which was compounded by the declining purchasing power of wages for those who remained in formal employment (Ferguson 1999). Many laid-off miners had to secure their livelihoods in the informal economy, as petty traders or squatters on mine land, engaged in vegetable gardening.

The privatisation process thus empowered certain social groups and disempowered others. In particular, it marginalised and excluded the mineworkers, who had been integral to the Zambian economy and politics, from the new processes of wealth creation, even as their efforts, to maintain their livelihoods as squatter farmers posed a further barrier to economic rationalisation. Many mineworkers suffered from depression as a consequence of these changes and left the challenge of earning a living to their enterprising wives (Field Notes 2002). The increased economic role that women began to play in their communities and households had implications for gender relations as women became more assertive in budgetary decision-making in their homes. While many miners had been allowed to buy their mine houses as part of the privatisation process, most miners who lost their jobs have since resold them and moved into low-income compounds where housing is self-made and precarious at best. Thus, the economic status of former miners was rendered extremely precarious by the privatisation process. Moreover, the vaunted identity of miners has been undermined, and they have become just another underpaid workforce, unable, as one miner said, to aspire even to buying a car or a fridge (Field Notes 2002).

As other scholars have argued, programmes aimed at the creation of free markets undermine popular democratic participation as well as livelihoods. Mkandawire has going so far as to refer to the post-structural adjustment African states as 'choiceless democracies' (Wignaraja 1993; Mkandawire and Soludo 1999). Indeed, the deregulation of markets aimed at limiting the role of the state in the economy and the privatisation of collectively held national assets, which are hallmarks of neoliberal restructuring, deter the deepening of democratic participation by the majority of citizens especially in relation to decision-making about economic policy. Rather than empowering citizens by freeing up private engagement in production and expanding entrepreneurial opportunities, the result has been to transfer the means of production – including large, strategic public assets – into private hands, foreign as well as domestic. It is within this context that we have seen a resurgence of peasant social movements in countries like Zambia, often emerging as a response to social, economic and political marginalisation. In Zambia (as elsewhere), such social movements reflect new sets of social, economic and political demands in response to the new identities and class positions resulting from neoliberal restructuring. I turn now to present a case study of one such movement, the Luana Famers' Cooperative, beginning first with a discussion of landownership and use, and changes to relevant legislation. As we shall see, such changes set the stage for the formation of the Cooperative and subsequent activism taken up by the group.

The Luana Farmers' Cooperative

When the state-owned Zambian copper mines were sold to transnational mining corporations, the workforce was cut from 62,000 employees to 25,000 employees (Kaunda 2002). Many of the laid-off mineworkers had no other skills and nowhere to turn, so they began to engage in agricultural activities on state-owned marginal forest land near urban centres such as Kitwe, Luanshya and Chingola. Their farming was mainly for subsistence and also generated a small surplus of vegetables and maize for local markets. Small-scale production for urban markets was already an established practice by squatters who had migrated to the Copperbelt looking for mining jobs and seen as legitimate in the popular imagination. Some farmed in share-cropping arrangements (rent was paid in produce to the landowner) while others paid annual rent to the title holders, but a growing number of people simply farmed without legal title on lands owned by the state-owned mining company (ZCCM) as well as state-owned forested lands (Oxfam Communique 1998). Historically, governments had allowed for miners' relatives, visitors and job seekers to engage in subsistence farming on these lands in times of high unemployment; however, the privatisation process put the squatters' access to land in question. In response, displaced miners near Chingola created the Luana Farmers' Cooperative, which soon led a new struggle for subsistence rights against the state and national elites.

The sale of Zambia's copper mines was but one part of the broader liberalisation programme that sought to establish private property rights over state ownership and collective use of many of Zambia's most valuable assets, including farmland. Few countries in Africa liberalised their agricultural sector more quickly or thoroughly than Zambia after 1991. Indeed, it is often commented that Zambia underwent the 'speediest' privatisation programme in Africa. The government's land privatisation initiative, at the behest of the international financial institutions, aimed to restructure the agricultural sector to be more globally competitive and market oriented. The success of Kenya and other African economies in exporting new agricultural products such as flowers to Europe inspired the Zambian Government to encourage similar production on Zambia's plentiful agricultural land, and the country's economic elite also saw the potential for developing a horticulture industry for new global markets. Much of the land for such agro-industries, however, was already under squatter cultivation. Through their contacts in the state, prospective large-scale horticulturalists began to campaign for changes in the Lands Act, so expanses of state land could be sold and brought under commercial production. Zambia's elite thought the country's future would be in export-oriented agricultural production (Hansungule, Feeney, and Palmer 1998). These demands coincided with the land pressures generated by lay-offs in the mining industry and the general poor performance of the local economy in the Copperbelt region.

When ZCCM was privatised, the surrounding land they held was transferred to the new mine owners, and it was inevitable that the new mine owners would seek to clear the land of its occupants to undertake further exploration and mine development. In addition, some of the privatised land would enter the commercial market and could be used for horticultural purposes. According to Oxfam, an estimated 15,000–20,000 squatter farmers living on mine lands in Chingola, 15,000 in Kitwe, and about 50,000 in the remaining mining towns of Nchanga, Mufulira, Nkana, Luanshya and Konkola would be displaced as a result (Hansungule, Feeney, and Palmer 1998). A World Bank programme laid out clear guidelines for resettling squatters or persons affected by mine development (World Bank 1990), but the new mine owners were slow to comply and in many cases underestimated the impact on communities (Environmental Manager, ZCCM 2002). In a number of cases, the mining companies demanded that squatters be removed on the grounds that they were situated on unsafe land, in one case suggesting that the unplanned settlement was on a tailings dam (Mpishi 2002). To help push them out, the company discontinued the squatters' access to water. In many cases, such action by new mine owners meant the Zambian Government had to pick between protecting access to land for its citizens, who desperately needed it for survival, and enforcing the private property rights of the new mine owners. To maintain its credibility with investors, the national state often acted in support of the transnational mining companies' claims. Frequently, this breached rulings by local councils seeking to protect long-standing unplanned settlements, whose inhabitants maintained their land claims based on the long period during which the state had not acted to evict them, allowing them to establish fairly permanent infrastructure.

In 1994, the government introduced new land legislation, which passed in 1995 after significant debate and amendments as the new Lands Act 1995. Its purpose was to liberalise land holding, thereby allowing for the purchase of what was categorised as 'unused land'. Until then, land had not been viewed as a commodity to be bought and sold for private gain but as a resource available to those who cultivated it to meet their subsistence needs. For instance, under the 1975 Lands Act, all land belonged to the people of Zambia and was held in trust by the state. This began to change in the early 1990s. First, the Land Acquisition Act of 1990 permitted acquisition of underdeveloped land without payment or compensation. The next major change came with the new land legislation in 1995. This legislation moved towards privatising and commodifying agricultural land by simplifying the land holding system, abolishing a number of categories of land tenure to retain just two: customary (allocating use rights through consultation with the local chief and local authority, but permitting such holdings to be converted to statutory) and statutory (full private ownership permitting land to be sold) and (Hansungule, Feeney, and Palmer 1998). The main objective was to remove all obstacles to the process of land alienation and to attach commercial value to underdeveloped and unused land; the new legislation was silent as to the rights of squatters and criminalised new land invasions. It set up a complex, expensive and overly centralised formal process for acquiring land that involved tendering an application to a

Commissioner of Lands situated in the capital city, Lusaka. One could obtain title to land, then, only if one could successfully navigate the process and absorb the costs associated with it, which privileged Zambian elites with no previous ties to the land over those who farmed it for subsistence, such as the former copper miners. In time, Zambian elites began to lay claim to vast tracts of land, some of which was already being farmed, with many former miners and other subsistence farmers subsequently forcibly evicted. There was a dispute settlement process under a Land Tribunal to address multiple claims to land, but again, it was complex, expensive and overly centralised, thus in practice accessible mainly to those with substantial financial resources.

Where necessary, the new landholders deployed the state's coercive machinery to force the squatter farmers off the land, precipitating confrontations that in some cases led to loss of life. In response, there were massive, spontaneous mobilisations against the expropriations in Chingola, Luana and other communities on the Copperbelt. The squatter farmers began to organise themselves to take political action to defend the land, and through such a process, the Luana Farmers' Cooperative was formed. The Luana Farmers' Cooperative set up a surveillance system to alert them to the actions of the new landowners and confronted surveyors and local police accompanying the new landowners when they ventured onto the previously state-controlled forest lands. Some group members even took to bearing arms in an effort to defend the land they were working, all of which intensified the confrontations over a period of months in 2001 and 2002 (Kapele 2002). At its peak, the Luana Farmers' Cooperative was said to have organised over 6000 squatter and other local farmers, many of whom were women.

The physical confrontations drew public and political attention to the plight of the displaced farmers, and local town officials and national representatives began to respond to their demands. To further their influence, the Cooperative shifted towards political advocacy, taking on a formal structure by electing an executive and a spokesperson. The leadership decided that in order to protect squatters against periodic attacks from the new absentee landowners, they needed to have the government certify their claim to the land they had been farming. Thus, the Cooperative began to organise campaigns involving sending hundreds of farmers to authorities to regularise their land tenure (Kapele 2002). When the authorities were unresponsive, they began a series of occupations of the Town Clerk's Office demanding land titles. These confrontations shifted their focus to members of parliament, some of whom changed sides and began advocating for the farmers (Kapele 2002). The MPs and MMD officials were attentive to the upcoming national elections, noting they would have to contend with a well-organised group of local residents who had the sympathy of their communities.

Eventually, the state began to relent and slowly begin to grant the squatter farmers title to their land, first with lands that were uncontested and then the contested lands, which required some form of adjudication. The process was not altogether smooth, and the squatter farmers were required to pay for their own land survey in order for their titles to be processed. For many, the cost was prohibitive. Cooperative members received some financial support in their land title claims from international non-governmental organisations such as Oxfam-UK, which worked through Oxfam-Zambia, in addition to pooling their own funds (Kapele 2002; Lunga 2002). The land claimants also were subjected to a convoluted process that involved the Ministry of Lands, the Ministry of Agriculture and the Ministry of Forests, all of which had to cede their claims to the land before the title could be processed by the town council bureaucracy. The process was further hampered by periodic breakdowns in the bureaucratic system during 2001–2002. For instance, the City Council workers in Kitwe walked off the job for four months in 2001 because they had not been paid for the previous five months.

The outcome of the conflict, then, was largely determined by the collective mobilisations of the squatter farmers. But it was also mediated by the political and economic context – the political success of the Cooperative coincided with the collapse of the European flower trade because too many cultivators had already entered the market. A corresponding consideration was that the Zambian elites were not able to access enough capital for the infrastructure needed to make them competitive internationally, and many began to abandon their farms. The very logic of global competitiveness that had seduced them now turned on them, opening space for local considerations to come to the fore.

Understanding resistance from below

The Luana Farmers' Cooperative exhibits a moderate level of organisation and tactical ingenuity, pursuing short-term objectives rooted in survival strategies that seek to facilitate access to land for subsistence. The case study suggests that the Luana farmers' collective action represented what Moyo (2002, 2) has termed 'basic socio-political organisation (mobilised) to defend the mere social reproduction of the peasantry'. This simple demand implied complex changes in the emerging regulatory regime – they pushed for policy reforms and social changes in land tenure, the administration of land distribution processes, agricultural policies such as subsidies on fertilisers and infra-structural investment. In pursuit of their goals, they engaged a range of familiar tactics, including labour pooling, resource pooling, petitions, demonstrations, visits to offices of the District Commissioner and Mayor and to local members of parliament, letter writing, lobbying, information sharing and engaging in electoral mobilisation. While not seeking political control over the state, these struggles represent a profound challenge to the norms of globalising capitalism championed by the state. This rural–urban peasant resistance made short-term demands, not only seeking to meet basic economic needs but also sought to re-establish state accountability to society and thus a new relationship between the two. The demands for political and social rights led to some measure of success in that challenging the state altered the management of land alienation and distribution.

The Luana Farmers' Cooperative not only represented a reaction to neoliberal economic development, but it also presupposed a commitment to modernist values rooted in claims for subsistence rights to livelihood, food security and access to clean water, shelter, clothing and minimal public health, to be guaranteed by the state (Milner 2002). The claims mirror the aspirations of national welfare state/developmentalist regimes that predated the neoliberal globalisation order, which, in the case of Zambia, were articulated through the concept of Zambian humanism. These kinds of claims now find resonance with the international commitments to the Millennium Development Goals and the World Bank's focus on poverty reduction as the impetus for development, all of which are consistent with the idea of human rights as a global value. Indeed, the Luana Farmers' Cooperative and similar locally based social movements are making rights claims that force them to engage with sections of the Zambia state, even though as land squatters, they sought to deny certain legally sanctioned property rights and thus defy other aspects of state regulation.

Struggles of local social movements have become widespread in post-independence, neoliberal Southern Africa. A sizeable body of literature now exists that optimistically presents these local social movements as part of a broader phenomenon of rights-based resistance to the precarious conditions created by late twentieth-century global capitalism, mobilised by communities acting collectively to secure their material well-being, economic control and place-bounded identity (Bradbury 1987; Mahmoud and Moyo 2002; Moyo and Yeros 2005; Wignaraja 1993; Oxfam Communique 1998). These developments have generated a diversity of local movements, from the more organised to the spontaneous; from rural to urban to in-between, that utilise a variety of ideologies, strategies and tactics. While they may share a social basis for action – responding to predatory capitalist expansion – they have different capacities and tendencies for political action. Some have become more militant in pursuing their claims for land, using land occupation as a tactic, while others have engaged more traditional methods of resistance.

These movements draw on local knowledge to construct identities of resistance through particularistic claims that simultaneously challenge the logic of competitive global capitalism. Thus, their potential is much deeper than their short-term objectives and is connected to the social, economic and political rejection of the neoliberal consensus. Moyo and Yeros go so far as to present formations such as this as representing 'the nucleus of anti-imperialist politics today ... [which] is to be found in the countrysides of the periphery' (2005, 9). While there is limited evidence of widespread 'class consciousness' as driving their emergence, the claims the Cooperative have made are consistent with the tendency towards demanding democratic accountability from states and local authorities for the distribution of resources and access to services and investment. They also invoke the human rights principles, claiming subsistence rights, land rights and protection from the arbitrary actions of powerful elites, within a liberal democratic modernist frame that presupposes the universality of the international human rights principles.

The suggestion that movements like the Luana Farmers' Cooperative may be able to build from anti-hegemonic to counter-hegemonic movements is predicated on the centrality of land struggles and livelihood issues to the lived contradictions of the neoliberal globalist order. In the Zambian case, they embody demands for social protection that challenge the legitimacy of the neoliberal project. These local resistance movements are mobilised, as in other communities that are subject to the precarious conditions created by the articulations of early twentieth-century global capitalism, to secure the material well-being, economic control and the place-bounded identity of local communities (Bradbury 1987; Wignaraja 1993; Oxfam Communique 1998). They also represent a potential articulation of an alternative vision of economic development that is grounded in social and ecological sustainability as well as meeting material needs. Whether this amounts to counter-hegemonic agency remains very much an open question. If these practices, incubated in local, marginal places, can be disseminated, modelled or simply replicated in other theatres, they may inspire other anti-capitalist struggles. They have the potential to mature into broadly based movements making radical demands for equitable distribution of resources, plus guarantees of land and subsistence rights that test the prevailing power relations. As such, their efforts may lead to the reconstitution of modes of governance that include the priorities, needs and aspirations of local peoples, against the current corporate domination of decision-making based on market logics and lowest cost of production considerations. Nevertheless, it may be wise to not overstate their potential given that many remain largely ad hoc, conjectural and short-term in their demands on the state in response to socio-economic crisis.

Conclusion

In the final analysis, the resistance by squatter farmers to being displaced from their livelihoods and marginalised, or even erased, from the state's consciousness, represents a unique yet generalisable form of resistance against the form of predatory capitalist expansion that has become widespread in Southern Africa. It also demonstrated the potential for local claims to be sustained despite the shift of authority from the national to the global scale under globalising neoliberalism. The contradictions in the process provided opportunities for local mobilisations and collective action, and a reassertion of local agency that should have implications for the neoliberal project.

Increasingly in the neoliberal era, the African state is called upon, not to provide social protection as a right of citizenship but to guarantee private property rights for national elites and foreign capital. That the locus of conflict often is between local community collectives and foreign multinational corporations, each asserting their claim to state protection or enforcement of their rights to the resource, further complicates the prospect that the state will be able to mediate. To date, a narrow conception of rights has accompanied neoliberal restructuring, such that new definitions of citizenship depart substantially from the anti-colonial notions of citizenship articulated during the liberation struggle and immediately after independence. The primacy of the national identity, which gives force even to the notion that an economy can be organised to compete with other economies, has been undermined by the rejection of claims for shared, equal rights in favour of the imposition of obligation in a manner reminiscence of the colonial era when an individual or community's relationship to the state was defined by what tribute or dues they owed to it, with little or no reciprocal claim. The shift to neoliberalism and the imposition of self-regulating markets has been met by a set of counterclaims based on values and expectations developed for a generation under the socialist-inspired national development projects that were central to the mobilisation of new post-colonial identities, nationalisms and legitimacy for post-independence regimes. In the case of Zambia, not only were the new demands for user fees for social and municipal services counterposed against the values of the Zambian humanist political project of the UNIP government, but they also challenged the very assumptions that underlay the struggle for political reform in the late 1980s and early 1990s.

At a political level, the instrumental notions of democracy and citizenship that emerged after 1991 were met by a mobilised citizenry insisting that democracy includes socio-economic, cultural and environmental rights. I would suggest that, to a certain extent, that condition is generalised across Southern Africa as nation-states struggle with the pressures globalisation imposes on the nationalist project. Not only are notions of citizenship in flux, but so too is the role of the state and with it certain key operating assumptions about the democratisation processes that proliferated on the continent in the early 1990s. Despite the widespread adoption of neoliberal economic programmes and limited democratising measures, the longer-term socio-economic vision for the continent is still very much an open question.

Funding

This work was supported by the International Development Research Centre (IDRC).

References

Bradbury, John. 1987. "Strategies in Local Communities to Cope with Industrial Restructuring." In *Labour, Environment and Industrial Change*, edited by G. J. R. Linge and G. A. van der Knaap, 167–184. London: Routledge.

Environmental Manager. 2002. "ZCCM-IH, Interview."

Ferguson, James. 1999. *Expectations of Modernity: Myths and Meanings of Urban Life on the Zambian Copperbelt*. Berkeley: University of California Press.

Hansungule, Michelo, Patricia Feeney, and Robin Palmer. 1998. *Report on the Land Tenure Insecurity on the Zambian Copperbelt*. Lusaka: Oxfam GB in Zambia.

Kapele, Mr. 2002. "Chairman, Mulema Farm Cooperative, Interview, Luana, Zambia."

Kaunda, Francis. 2002. *Selling the Family Silver: The Zambian Copper Mines Story*. Kwazulu-Natal: Interpak Books.

Lunga, John. 2002. "Interview, Oxfam-Zambia."

Mahmoud Ben Romdhane, and Sam Moyo, eds. 2002. *Peasant Organizations and the Democratization Process in Africa*. Dakar: CODESERIA.

Milner, Wesley. 2002. "Economic Globalization and Rights: An Empirical Analysis." In *Globalization and Human Rights*, edited by Alison Brysk, 77–97. Berkeley: University of California Press.

Mkandawire, Thandika, and Charles Soludo. 1999. *Our Continent, Our Future: African Perspectives on Structural Adjustment*. Dakar: CODESRIA.

Moyo, Sam. 2002. "Peasant Organizations and Rural Civil Society in Africa: An Introduction." In *Peasant Organizations and the Democratization Process in Africa*, edited by Mahmoud Ben Romdhane and Sam Moyo, 1–26. Dakar: CODESERIA.

Moyo, Sam, and Paris Yeros, eds. 2005. "The Resurgence of Peasant Movements under Neo-liberalism." In *Reclaiming the Land*, edited by Sam Moyo, and Paris Yeros, 1–64. London: Zed Books.

Mpishi, Alex. 2002. "Interview. Environmental Officer, Mopani Copper Mines."

Oxfam Communique. 1998. *Land Tenure Insecurity on the Zambian Copperbelt*. December 3. London: Oxfam United Kingdom

Radfield, Robert R. 1956. *Peasant Society and Culture*. Chicago: University of Chicago Press.

Wignaraja, Ponna. 1993. "Rethinking Development and Democracy." In *New Social Movements in the South: Empowering the People*, edited by Poona Wignaraja, 4–35. London: Zed Books.

World Bank. 1990. *Operational Directive 4.30 – Involuntary Resettlement*. Washington, DC: World Bank.

Wulf, Jürgen. 1988. "Zambia under the IMF Regime." *African Affairs* 87 (349): 579–594.

Geologies of power: blood diamonds, security politics and Zimbabwe's troubled transition

Richard Saunders

Department of Political Science, York University, Toronto, ON, Canada

The article shows how the 2006 discovery of significant deposits of diamonds in eastern Zimbabwe transformed the minerals sector and its nascent regional business networks, with significant political implications. It argues that diamond revenues have been used to prop up the ruling Zimbabwe African National Union – Patriotic Front (ZANU-PF) party and maintain its hold on the state and dominance in the Government of National Unity. Internal battles over control of and access to diamonds posed a direct challenge to the viability of the new, 'power-sharing' unity government and prospects for a democratic transition in Zimbabwe. Because profits from mining are benefiting security forces and factions of the ZANU-PF elite, Zimbabwe's diamonds have cemented political corruption, further marginalised the two opposition parties, and may have guaranteed election victory for ZANU-PF in the country's next election.

Introduction

In 2006, major new alluvial diamond deposits were discovered in Marange District in eastern Zimbabwe. The discovery coincided with a dramatic and worsening economic crisis of accumulation and political crisis of legitimacy for interests associated with the ruling ZANU-PF party and state. The result by 2007 was a new case of 'blood diamonds', whereby state security forces secretly oversaw the extraction and criminal smuggling of rough diamonds – in the process, violently displacing local communities, informal miners and legal title-holders, and depriving the national treasury of significant new revenues and foreign exchange earnings. Unlike other infamous cases like Sierra Leone and Angola, where the illicit trade in diamonds helped fuel armed rebellion, Zimbabwe's conflict diamonds came to pose a threat to legitimate government from within. Following the 2008 national elections and the subsequent formation of a Government of National Unity (GNU) in 2009, corruption and criminality associated with Marange diamonds negatively inflected the trajectory of Zimbabwe's fragile national political transition. The GNU, inaugurated in February 2009, brought ZANU-PF together with two opposition parties: Movement for Democratic Change-Tsvangirai (MDC-T) and Movement for Democratic Change-Mutambara. It also included some new institutions for monitoring and facilitating the GNU and furthering the transition towards the next government in 2013, as well as provisions for drafting and finalising a new democratic constitution. Soon, however, the convergence of political need and elite accumulation opportunities in Marange's alluvial diamond geology came to pose a direct challenge to the viability of the new 'unity' government. Blood diamonds emerged as a stark litmus test of its success.

In Zimbabwe, the emergence of criminalised networks spanning political, security and business elites – and national borders – raises important questions about the shape of and prospects for transitions to post-nationalist political orders in southern Africa. After the decades long establishment of thickly woven political–security–business networks, cemented through corrupt forms of accumulation, it is unclear whether heavily circumscribed political transitions and the weakened state forms they produce are sufficient to deliver new kinds of participatory politics and economies. Are states, such as Zimbabwe, already weakened by neoliberal reform capable of mounting challenges to embedded elite interests, particularly when the latter include elements from the official and unofficial securitocracy? In more profound terms, is a post-nationalist political-*economic* order possible?

This article will explore these broader issues by focusing on the role played by Marange's diamonds in exacerbating elite struggles within ZANU-PF and in sharpening conflict among the GNU's main partners, a situation which undermined the chances for a political transition to a more transparent, accountable and democratic government. At the same time, the reach and implications of Marange's diamond trade extends beyond the country's borders. As we shall see, Zimbabwe's blood diamonds provide a lens into the dynamics, extent and wider implications of criminalised political-cum-business accumulation networks in southern Africa. The minerals sector is a particularly important point of investigation given both its comparative productive value in several countries of the region and the latters' documented involvement in illegal trading networks. Mining also reflects the ambiguous and complex interface between local governments and elites, and international markets and regulatory institutions such as the Kimberley Process Certification Scheme (KP), the worldwide association of government, industry and civil society interests that were established in 2003 to develop, monitor and enforce standards for the mining and export of rough diamonds. If, as the Zimbabwe case suggests, key levers to encourage transparency, equitable participation in production and the rule of law like the KP are weak or unreliable, then a more critical analysis is needed for assessing and combating an entrenched, criminalised and elite-driven politics.

Mining, politics and power in Zimbabwe

Zimbabwe's minerals sector has been an important source of capital accumulation, political contestation and policy intervention by the state since the first years of independence. Mining's unique production characteristics set it apart from other leading sectors like manufacturing, where structural adjustment devastated local businesses in the 1990s, and commercial agriculture, which was transformed by ZANU-PF's militant project of 'fast track' land reform in the 2000s. In mining, a different set of factors has been crucial to the development of the industry: the availability of comparatively large sums of investment capital, access to foreign exchange for inputs, spares and skills, and support from surrounding infrastructure. While other key economic sectors suffered during the structural adjustment years of the 1990s, mining experienced growth fuelled primarily by international companies. By the end of the 1990s, Zimbabwe seemed poised to become a significant force in African mining. New gold sector investments lifted the country into third place among African gold producers and into the top 10 in the world, and a US $500m investment in platinum established a major new foreign currency earner. Other mining sectors, including ferrochrome, coal and nickel, were also resurgent.

As other productive sectors were rendered unstable for the acquisitive, faction-ridden and internally competitive political and business elite, minerals emerged as a central point of contention. Not only did larger scale mining, dominated by gold and increasingly by platinum, offer high foreign currency denominated returns, but also it figured centrally in factional struggles for political ascendancy within ZANU-PF, serving as a barometer of sorts marking the sway of different factions of the party hierarchy in their struggles to amass political and economic capital. However, the first year of the 2000s saw the collapse of most large-scale mining, notably the crucial gold sector, as shortages or inconsistent supplies of foreign currency, fuel, electricity and spares led to dramatic scale backs of production and in many cases, the mothballing and effective closure of primary production (Saunders 2008). The decline of the gold sector was emblematic of the difficulties faced in the wake of production constraints and increasingly chaotic government administration of the sector. In 1999–2001, 15 gold mines were closed or mothballed, and gold exports and earnings dropped sharply (BusinessMap 2001, 30). By 2003, gold production, at 12.5 tonnes, was less than half what it had been in 1999 and by 2008 most commercial operations had stalled, with output falling to 3.5 tonnes, the lowest levels since before independence (Zimbabwe Chamber of Mines 2009, 23–25).

Meanwhile, a rapid erosion of bureaucratic professionalism and authority within government underscored a wider undermining of the 'rule of law'. The ruling party leadership came under the growing influence of a security-led political strategy rooted in militarist and commandist management of government, and state institutions were increasingly subordinated to partisan considerations (Hammar and Raftopoulos 2003; Raftopoulos 2009; Saul and Saunders 2005). Disjointed, unpredictable and often contradictory regulations and announcements by different state agencies and officials signalled growing policy-making competition among interests inside and outside designated regulatory institutions. Key players affected included the Reserve Bank of Zimbabwe (RBZ) and the state's primary mining-related institutions, the Zimbabwe Mining Development Corporation (ZMDC) (the state's mine operator), the Minerals Marketing Corporation of Zimbabwe (MMCZ) (the agency in charge of minerals sales and exports), and ministerial departments concerned with issues of direct investment and 'indigenisation' or black economic empowerment. These state mining structures were directly drawn into intense factional struggles within the ruling party, deeply eroding coherence in formal policy-making processes (Saunders 2007, 2009).

This murky terrain was further complicated in 2002, with the imposition of sanctions by the European Union, the USA and most western donor nations that targeted leading figures in ZANU-PF, the security forces and businesspeople who had been implicated in political violence, human rights abuses and the rigging of the 2002 Presidential election. Following the suspension of lending by key international financial institutions and donors in 1998 and ensuing local shortages of foreign exchange, the personal sanctions of 2002 effectively cut off much of the political and business elite from external sources of financing and sharply undermined their trading and cross-border commercial activities. So while many established mining houses looked to sell their Zimbabwe investments in an environment of stalled production and uncertain long-term property rights, the opportunities for local mining takeovers were sharply limited by shortages of hard currency needed to sustain production, and threats of diminished market access for exports. Targeted sanctions, which included the ZMDC, further weakened ZANU-PF's mining restructuring options. In particular, assembling international financial support for locally driven mining house takeovers became nearly impossible after the imposition of sanctions.

These constraints opened the way for new foreign players with the political and financial resources needed to ensure investment security, namely, investors based in southern Africa (and later, China) with links to regional political interests supportive of ZANU-PF. New mining investors were led by prominent South African Black Economic Empowerment activists, including Mzi Khumalo, Bridget Radebe and Patrice Motsepe, and by politically linked regional entrepreneurs like Mwana Africa (Saunders 2008). Investors also included two traditional players, South Africa's Implats and the global conglomerate Anglo-American, both of which aimed to secure new investments by means of 'empowerment credits' negotiated with government. So while ZANU-PF's assertive nationalist rhetoric facilitated significant ownership transfer to blacks – 'black empower-ment' – paradoxically, in the first year of the 2000s, those empowered were largely expatriate Africans. There were few positive examples of new black Zimbabwean mining houses and ZANU-PF-linked businesspeople taking stakes; indeed, the leading black Zimbabwean mining entrepreneur of the late 1990s, Mutumwa Marere, fell out with the ruling party, suffered the seizure of his assets through 'specification' by government and was nudged into self-exile in South Africa. At the same time, the arrival of Southern African investors laid the groundwork for closer regional integration of mining entrepreneurs with complementary linkages to powerful political and security constitu-encies in neighbouring countries. These dynamics in Zimbabwean mining – the frustrated accumulation ambitions of elites amid their rising needs, moribund if not declining output and emergence of nascent cross-border business networks – were dramatically transformed by the discovery of substantial new mineral assets in 2006.

Marange diamonds: a new political geography over old fault lines

In 2006, significant deposits of alluvial diamonds became known in Chief Chiadzwa's area of Marange District, in south-east Zimbabwe. The public revelation of easily accessible surface diamonds that could be retrieved through non-mechanised mining (including hand digging and panning) presented opportunities for important new mining ventures at low cost. Soon, a massive 'diamond rush' had descended on Chiadzwa (Saunders 2007; Sachikonye 2007). But this rush was not spontaneous. It is argued here that while a broad range of interests sought their fortune through diamonds, the Zimbabwean Government and elite political interests manoeuvred to control both the legal and illegal diamond trade. When state security agencies moved in late 2006 to impose control over illegal informal mining and diamond trading, it soon became apparent that ZANU-PF's aim was not to eliminate the black market diamond trade, but rather, to facilitate and incorporate such trade within a mining regime dominated by elements of ZANU-PF's security and political leadership. A secretive alliance of political and economic interests soon converged around Marange's resources: soldiers, policeman and low-level security officers on the ground, ranking security and political officials, informal miners, local and expatriate black market traders, and state mining operators.

From the start of the diamond rush, diamonds and national politics were inextricably linked in a bloody cocktail of power.

Diamonds represented a potential windfall for those who controlled access to them, creating a powerful dynamic of conflict and competition among a variety of actors. These actors included the legal title-holder to the Chiadzwa claim from April 2006, African Consolidated Resources plc (ACR), a British-registered company led by mostly white Zimbabwean nationals, state regulatory and producer structures, such as RBZ, ZMDC and MMCZ, leading state security agencies, including the Zimbabwean National Army (ZNA), Zimbabwe Republic Police (ZRP) and Central Intelligence Organisation (CIO), which were soon tasked with securing the diamond fields, political and allied local business elites, informal or 'illicit' miners (known as 'magweja'), and the profoundly impoverished rural communities surrounding the diamond-bearing areas (Nyamunda and Mukwambo 2012). In particular, ACR had staked a claim to the mining title for an important section of the fields, pegged off and fenced a test mining section and begun preliminary surface operations by mid-2006. But ACR's control over the fields was cast in doubt soon after the prospect of a major find became publicly known.

Marange deposits represented an important opportunity for government and key state institutional players to reassert ministerial political control over an unquantified resource, and re-establish political influence in a region where the opposition MDC-T was prominent. Small-scale production held the promise of rapid accumulation for local business and political elites beset by deepening economic crisis, particularly because of the promise of foreign currency earnings from diamonds. Small-scale panners in the thousands saw the prospect of unregulated mining as a critical source of income for the survival of their households and communities, and according to some reports already had emerged as a problem for ACR in the first half of 2006 (Nyamunda and Mukwambo 2012, 9). Further, senior and lower ranking members of the state security agencies increasingly recognised the financial and political value of diamonds, whether mined legally under the ZMDC or illegally by syndicates, panners and forced labour.

In the context of contested legal claims and weakened state regulatory agencies, government officials intervened in a succession of linked moves to assert control over Marange. First, the erstwhile title-holder, ACR, was displaced by legal and political manoeuvres, and the resulting chaos provided government with an opportunity to forcefully 'restore order' over this national resource. In September 2006, Deputy Minister of Mines Tinos Rusere visited the area, announced that ACR's claim was invalid and invited informal miners to work the land, as long as they sold their rough diamonds to the parastatal MMCZ (Mukumbira 2006). This ignited a massive and increasingly chaotic diamond rush. Some reports (Hawkins 2009, 14) suggested that by October as many as 20,000 informal miners had descended on the diamond fields in just weeks, creating pandemonium and nurturing a thriving illegal buyers market, particularly because the cash-strapped MMCZ was unable to compete with illegal traders to purchase the stones. Government soon seized on the chaos and reasserted its control under the guise of protecting a strategic national resource. Thus began a period of recurrent and increasingly lethal violence in the diamond fields, perpetrated by state security agencies and lasting more than two years. (see Human Rights Watch 2009; Partnership Africa Canada 2009a; Zimbabwe Lawyers for Human Rights et al. 2009).

In November 2006, the government launched the first of several military-style interventions, ostensibly designed to restore order and legality to Marange's fields.

Operation *Chikorokoza Chapera* ('end to illegal panning') saw approximately 600 ZRP officers brutally evict diggers and impose a seal on the area, while forcing ACR to abandon its preliminary mining operations. More than 22,000 people were arrested nationwide – 9000 or more in Marange alone – though it appeared many of those arrested had no connection to the diamond trade (Human Rights Watch 2009, 19). Allegations soon emerged that police personnel were working with illegal miners in the secured zone by permitting access through bribes and commissions, and even digging for themselves. Senior government and military people were also implicated in diamond dealing (Saunders 2007). One domestic commentator wrote in 2007 of the manipulated chaos:

> our government will console itself with the thought that diamonds extracted from Marange have not been used to finance conflict. That does not make them clean because the gems have become a means by which senior government officials and their cronies have continued to acquire illicit wealth.

The source of the diamond fields mess, the writer continued, was government itself, and if the state had 'mobilised to clean up the mess in an exercise meant to portray government as working for the betterment of the country', it was a mess of its own deliberate making, enabling a solution of a decidedly self-interested and lucrative kind (*Zimbabwe Independent*, 1 June 2007).

Growing awareness of Marange's value ignited intense competition within state structures as well. Jurisdictional claims by the Ministry of Mines and Mineral Development, the ministry responsible for the ZMDC and MMCZ, led to battles among government departments and state institutions, and among political-cum-business factions of the ruling party for which some government agencies appeared to be proxies, over management rights to the resource. The conflicts primarily involved struggles over access rights, rather than the matter of regularising Marange production to render it more efficient or transparent. The RBZ challenged (ultimately unsuccessfully) the mining and indigenisation ministries' capacity to manage production and exports, and warned of large losses of potential income to the national treasury. Meanwhile, the mining ministry tightened control over the diamond activities of its state mining and marketing agencies amid a swirl of controversy, as senior officials connected to the state security sector and politically connected individuals were discovered attempting to smuggle large quantities of diamonds. Those arrested and charged included a government department director (since deceased) and the son of the CEO of Zimbabwe Defence Industries, a security-dominated firm active in the Democratic Republic of the Congo (DRC) and allegedly involved in illegal resource exploitation there (*Zimbabwe Independent*, 2 March 2007). By mid-2007, the foundations of a new and increasingly shadowy regime of Marange management were in place under the control of security-linked production networks. The state security forces' key role was underpinned by Chiadzwa's listing as a 'restricted area' under the Protected Places and Areas Act, with the ZRP given chief responsibility for securing the area. Meanwhile, the mining ministry moved to block the ACR's legal challenge over its title claims, and ramped up production through the ZMDC.

The new order was consolidated through renewed violence by security forces. Successive waves of attack in 2007–2008 led first by the police and later involving the ZNA and CIO subjected thousands of community members, local residents, informal miners, buyers and ordinary merchants and traders to severe legal and extralegal violence. The strategic aim of these attacks was not to stop the illegal trade, but rather to bring it under the control of the ruling party's political and security leadership. In this way, multiple networks of security-linked trading 'syndicates' emerged involving illegal miners, traders and security personnel. This arrangement seems to have been extraordinarily productive and lucrative; by 2008 Marange diamonds were appearing in markets as far-flung as Guyana, Sierra Leone, Dubai and India, and independent research suggested diamond syndicates were being consolidated and strengthened under the watch of government (Partnership Africa Canada 2009a, 2009b).

Election panic and violent consequences

The wider political significance of Marange's lucrative trade only became clear at the time of the 2008 national elections. Having lost the 29 March parliamentary elections (and the first round of the Presidential vote) to the MDC-T, ZANU-PF chose to fight its way back from the brink of political defeat through the use of extreme violence directed both at the opposition and traditional ZANU-PF constituencies that had broken rank with factions headed by Robert Mugabe (Human Rights Watch 2008). This path required both the loyalty of the active agents of ZANU-PF's political violence – the security forces, police, youth militias, 'war veterans' and others – and funding to facilitate their activities. Chiadzwa diamonds represented a key source of concealed cash financing and payment-in-kind for these security agencies. Marange's location in hotly contested Manicaland province (which had voted overwhelmingly for the MDC-T in the March elections) provided additional incentives for renewed action.

The immediate consequence was a series of deadly new interventions in Marange. The waves of violence unleashed in 2008 by state agencies against informal miners, traders, local communities, opposition supporters and activists and others had a double objective, to undermine electoral support for the MDC in the June round of voting and to consolidate control over diamond field revenues. Thus, the 2008 elections were a benchmark in the politicisation of Marange diamonds against the backdrop of organised political violence. 'Operation Restore Order', launched by the ZRP after the 29 March 2008 poll, claimed to target illegal miners and traders and seek re-establishment of government control in Marange. But the scope of violence was much wider. Thousands of local inhabitants were victimised in state-led violence, resulting in a cascade of serious human rights abuses including murder, severe beatings, rape and irregular detention (Zimbabwe Lawyers for Human Rights et al. 2009, 26–32). Violence associated with 'Restore Order' peaked before the June run-off vote but continued to simmer for months, and certainly well past the September 2008 signing of the Global Political Agreement (GPA), the political settlement involving ZANU-PF and the MDC formations. The GPA then set out the terms for the inclusion of the MDC into the government with ZANU-PF, establishing the GNU.

Reports of continued illegal mining and human rights abuses by the ZRP brought new pressures on, and responses from, the fragile GPA. ZANU-PF, which retained unilateral control of government ministries until February 2009, intensified its militarised involvement in the diamond fields by unleashing a new and profoundly violent assault on black market mining in late October 2008. This time the ZNA led the attack. Operation *Hakudzokwi* ('area of no return') culminated in unprecedented numbers of deaths and human rights abuses in Chiadzwa and surrounding areas. The ZNA's deployment of three brigades immediately led to massive violence against miners, traders, rural folk and occasionally even involved skirmishes with members of the Zimbabwean Police. Independent reports documented the shooting of informal miners from army helicopters and systematic illegal abductions, rapes and beatings by army personnel. During the 3-week period when the ZNA was solely in control of Chiadzwa, one influential report noted, 'thousands of gross human rights abuses occurred' there and in surrounding districts and at least 214 civilians were killed. By government's own account, tens of thousands of illegal miners were chased off the fields, and more than one thousand were arrested (Human Rights Watch 2009). However, the ZNA's tightened security regime in Chiadzwa failed to meet its officially stated goal of stopping the illegal trade in diamonds, and instead institutionalised and consolidated illicit mining under the control of the security forces and ZANU-PF sections of government, a grim reality later confirmed by documents leaked from the ZNA regional command (Brief for Sub-National 2010).

Widespread outrage following the revelation of gross human rights abuses under Operation *Hakudzokwi*, especially coming after the promise of shared power under the GPA, and led to new MDC and civil society calls for the demilitarisation, depoliticisation and regularisation of Marange diamonds. But dislodging the shadowy trading networks faced steep challenges in the context of 'shared power'. While the GPA promised greater transparency in government, it simultaneously created new incentives for entrenched political, security and business elites to defend their lucrative and strategic interests in Marange.

The GPA and stalled transitions: conflict diamonds in the time of democratisation

The GPA introduced a new dynamic into the political-economic matrix of Marange's conflict diamonds. On the one hand, the MDC's arrival in government diminished ZANU-PF's unmediated access to the state, and notably state finances[1]; on the other hand, this loss of access forced Robert Mugabe's party to defend existing and seek new off-budget sources of funding in order to sustain the partisan security-based bodies like the ZNA, ZRP and CIO, as well as youth militia and ZANU-PF youth, which had been key in retaining the presidency for ZANU-PF in 2008 and leveraging the negotiations leading to the GPA. A stark contradiction soon took root; the spirit and letter of the GPA came to stand as a primary challenge to the partisan illegal accumulation nexus at Marange, while the violent political strategy fuelled by its diamonds placed in doubt the GPA's goal of a political transition founded on a new democratic constitution and legitimate free and fair elections. ZANU-PF's continued political and economic profiting from diamonds required power-sharing to be undermined. Marange diamonds therefore emerged as a key 'litmus test' of the new GPA: if politicised illegal diamond networks could not be dislodged by the unity government, what hope was there for the wider 'normalisation' of the national political economy? (Saunders 2009).

The initial results were not encouraging. Soon after the GPA was signed in September 2008, violence and rights abuses perpetrated by state security agencies under Operation *Hokudzokwi* resumed, signalling an immediate challenge to the fragile political accords. The MDC was mostly silent on the issue, occupied until early 2009 with negotiations over the distribution of posts and power under the GPA. In this critical period leading up to the MDC's assumption of cabinet seats in February 2009, ZANU-PF used its control over the security forces and the Ministry of Mines and Minerals Development to seal off illegal diamond activities from wider GPA scrutiny and intervention, and shut down the flow of information from the fields. This situation persisted after the formation of the GNU when ZANU-PF strategically demanded and retained control of the mining ministry under Minister Obert Mpofu, along with key security ministries.

After the signing of the GPA, ZANU-PF's management of Marange continued to be characterised by secrecy and ministerial commandism. Through a series of measures, the party and its senior leadership further instrumentalised and subordinated the once-respected state mining bureaucracy, and in fact, the GNU 'partnership' itself. Minister Mpofu invoked ministerial discretion to impose personnel, plans and targets on ZMDC and MMCZ without consultation of MDC partners in government, the judicial system was deployed as a means of asserting ministry claims around ACR's title (and was ignored when unfavourable decisions were rendered), and information flows to, and collaboration with, other government ministries under MDC control were blocked. Longstanding requests from the local mining industry for Marange production figures remained unanswered. Others seeking information on diamond operations, the role of the security forces and related rights abuses, including local and international civil society organisations, were challenged, threatened, attacked and denied access to Marange. Even parliamentary structures were interfered with on Mpofu's instruction. As late as April 2010, fact-finding investigations by Parliament's Portfolio Committee on Mines, Energy and the Environment were blocked, its members repeatedly prevented from visiting Chiadzwa. The Minister cited spurious national security concerns as the reason (*The Standard*, 25 April 2010).

The extent and effectiveness of ZANU-PF's tight grip on Marange's management and the negative consequences of the MDC's marginalisation from decision-making within the GNU were drawn sharply into focus when the government confronted a challenge from the KP, of which Zimbabwe is a member (Kimberley Process n.d.). Marange had been a cause for concern within KP beginning with the initial diamond rush. As early as December 2006, important players within the KP like the World Diamond Council had raised queries about the irregular nature of production and legal title management in Chiadzwa. Initially, the focus was on the government's dispute and refutation of ACR's claim to legal title. Once reports of human rights abuses became known, the KP was requested to expand its investigation to include these as well. However, ministry officials deftly handled a KP mission that was dispatched in May–June 2007. The visiting team barely touched down; it flew over the Chiadzwa fields in a Zimbabwe Defence Forces helicopter, and saw few witnesses who had not been arranged by the ministry. The outcome was a report that gave a clean bill of health to a manifestly unhealthy situation (Kimberley Process 2007; Ziyera 2007). The firm and unobstructed hand of ministry and state security officials had proved effective in blunting the KP challenge, assisted by the KP's own internal weaknesses including lack of transparency, accountability, good faith and consensus among a diverse collection of industry, government and civil society members (Smillie 2010).

But the tide of international criticism following *Hakudzokwi* excesses in 2008 reignited KP concerns over smuggling, illegality and rights abuses. By early 2009, the government needed a more wide-ranging strategy to pre-empt Zimbabwe's possible suspension from the rough diamond trade by the KP. The ZANU-PF leadership pursued a multi-pronged initiative. This included lobbying regional government members of the KP, notably the Government of Namibia, the KP chair for 2009, clamping down on the information gathering and lobbying activities of civil society organisations investigating diamond abuses, and restructuring mining operations at Marange in ways that lent the appearance of legality in terms of the KP's minimum standards for fair diamond mining. Despite these measures, a new KP country review team visited Zimbabwe in mid-2009 and produced an interim report that was unusually harsh in its criticisms of government. The review team's confidential report called for the immediate demilitarisation of the diamond fields, the appointment of a Special Rapporteur to investigate allegations of human rights abuses, and the suspension of Marange diamond exports pending improvement of the situation (Kimberley Process 2009). But these potentially disastrous recommendations were kept under wraps, thanks in part to generous cooperation from ZANU-PF's erstwhile political ally, the Government of Namibia. Bernhard Esau, Namibia's Deputy Minister of Mines and KP Chair, oversaw a long delay in the publication of the review mission's interim report, and when it was leaked to the local media, he went to unusual lengths to blunt its sharper recommendations. Esau also helped set the stage for further manipulation of KP discussion of Marange in the lead-up to the organisation's annual plenary in Namibia in November 2009 (Human Rights Watch 2009; Nyaira 2009b). These actions sharply undermined the impact of the team's findings.

Meanwhile, ZANU-PF government officials mobilised the state media and security apparatus – also retained under ZANU-PF ministerial control in the GNU – to threaten key civil society organisations and individuals who had provided critical evidence to the KP mission. Minister Mpofu questioned the political motives of local groups, accusing non-governmental organisations (NGOs) of being 'deranged and requiring psychological examination' (in Bell 2009). State-controlled media served up warnings against future unpatriotic activity, and local community leaders, including Chief Newman Chiadzwa, who had been an impressive witness for the KP mission, were publicly harassed and accused of involvement in the illegal diamond trade. In Chief Chiadzwa's case, this intimidation allegedly led him to write a retraction of evidence he had supplied to the KP mission in June 2009 (Moyo 2009; Nyaira 2009a). Minister Mpofu also moved to counter KP detractors by purporting to regularise production at Marange through the introduction of new commercial joint venture mining operations. Again, ZANU-PF's unilateral control of ministry structures enabled opaque partisan management of this process of transition to commercialisation. In mid-2009, Mpofu secretly approved concessions for two new companies in Chiadzwa, Mbada Diamonds and Canadile Miners. Both involved joint ventures between the ministry's ZMDC and South African-based parent companies, and were presented with fanfare at the KP's November plenary as a reflection of government's attempt to bring Chiadzwa operations into compliance with KP standards. They won a favourable response from most KP members.

It was only after details of the joint venture deals emerged that new questions were raised about the motivation for, and beneficiaries of, the partnerships. The Mbada and Canadile concessions had troubling features in common; neither company was experi-enced in mining, let alone in the diamond sector, and both had direct links with Zimbabwean state security agencies, and by extension, ZANU-PF. Neither South Africa-based enterprise had been subjected to a transparent tendering process or undergone due diligence by the ZMDC in advance of their signing on with the Zimbabwean partner; indeed, by the ZMDC's own account, neither would have been likely to win a tendering process (Sixholo 2010). Moreover, while Minister Mpofu argued that the deals were rushed through because the government had been in urgent need of foreign exchange, there was little evidence that revenues had ended up in government's coffers – a situation which would become chronic by 2012, when it was reported that hundreds of millions of US dollars in proceeds due to government from the mining activities had not been deposited with the treasury (Partnership Africa Canada 2012). In reality, then, Mbada and Canadile reflected a strategic double move by ZANU-PF to deflect KP criticisms of illegal mining and rights abuses by normalising the institutional arrangements of Marange mining, without derailing the politicised administration and skewed financial benefits derived from it.

These combined ministerial interventions would succeed for the duration of the GPA, aided in part by the weak and uncertain positions of ZANU-PF's GPA partners. At the KP's annual plenary in November 2009, calls for Zimbabwe's immediate suspension were turned back. Zimbabwe agreed to a compromise, a Joint Work Plan and the appointment of a KP Monitor to assist the government in achieving KP certification compliance. NGO and media reports noted the role of Namibian, South African, Congolese, Tanzanian and Russian delegates in defusing the threats to Marange production, and indicated that the 'farcical' decision on Zimbabwe was causing a crisis of confidence in the KP for some of its key members (*Daily Telegraph* (UK), 5 November 2009; Gagnon 2009). Mpofu's spirited defence of the Marange mess, backed by political allies in the region and industry voices keen to see the diamonds on international markets, deflected debates away from the demonstrably irregular situation in Zimbabwe and onto the KP and its criteria and practices, even as new revelations seemed to confirm that ZANU-PF and its security and business allies' quest to lock down control over Marange's riches continued unabated in the wake of sustained criticism and KP threats (Nyaira 2010).

At the same time, criticism mounted within the KP about the Marange situation, with Zimbabwe becoming a central focus of deliberation in 2009 and 2010. The 'regularisation' of production through the Mbada and Canadile joint ventures failed to disguise a deeply troubling pattern of military and ZANU-PF partisan involvement in exploiting illicit diamonds. Independent research published in 2010 by KP founding members, Global Witness (2010) and Partnership Africa Canada (2010), documented ZANU-PF and security forces links to the Marange miners, highlighted how little diamond revenue was flowing into public coffers, and repeated calls for Zimbabwe's suspension from the rough diamond trade. The KP Monitor for Zimbabwe appointed in early 2010, Abbey Chikane from South Africa, was drawn into the mess. He ignored evidence of continuing rights abuses and irregular military involvement in mining, including authenticated reports from within the ZNA itself, and officially recommended in June 2010 that Marange diamonds be given the KP seal of approval for export (Chikane 2010). As a direct result of Chikane's engagement with the Centre for Research and Development, the leading diamond research organisation working on Marange and a KP civil society member organisation, their local civil society researchers were severely harassed. Its director, Farai Maguwu, was irregularly detained and harshly treated. The uproar that followed at the KP's semi-annual meeting, where Chikane's report was discussed, placed Chikane's own future as Zimbabwe monitor in jeopardy, and led to new calls by civil society partners and some member governments in the KP for reform and recalibration of the organisation's criteria for assessing the 'cleanliness' of rough diamond production. In the short term, the KP maintained its overall suspension of Marange diamond exports, but in the longer term the combined and complementary forces of economic interests, political allegiances and administrative authority overwhelmed those calling for greater transparency, equity and accountability in Marange, enabled in part by the KP's own internal institutional weaknesses, which were strategically preyed upon by ZANU-PF government officials. Simultaneously, voices in the GNU challenging the murky management of the rough diamond trade were blunted by ZANU-PF's unilateral engagement of the KP and its refusal to divulge information on Marange to its partners in government.

In 2010, the KP allowed two significant allotments of stockpiled Marange diamonds to be sold overseas; by mid-2011, concerted government lobbying at the KP and the assumption of the chairmanship of the organisation by political ally DRC saw new moves to unban rough diamond exports – first via an irregular decree by the KP's DRC chair; later, at the annual meeting of the KP, by consensus. In November 2011, the KP's ban was lifted on the sale of existing stockpiles of Marange diamonds and by implication, future irregularly contracted production. With the unblocking of international sales a flood of stones – and poorly monitored revenues – ensued, and evidence soon emerged to suggest that government had already overseen significant exports of non-compliant rough diamonds while working to lift the KP's sanctions. Exasperated at the failure of the KP to stand up to Zimbabwean officials and their industry and political allies, and noting the institutionalisation of security and partisan political interests responsible for past rights abuses within the commercialised diamond mining sector, some KP members, including founding member Global Witness, quit the organisation at the end of 2011 (Global Witness 2011).

If Zimbabwe represented the 'new face' of conflict diamonds, in which the main perpetrators of diamond–fuelled human, social and economic rights abuses were governments and their allies, not armed rebels, it seemed clear that new thinking, regulatory criteria and enforcement measures were needed to combat the changed dynamics and agents of conflict (Saunders 2010; Vircoulon 2010). Unlike infamous cases like Sierra Leone and Angola, where the illicit trade in diamonds helped fuel armed rebellion, Zimbabwe's conflict diamonds allowed a party to a GNU to undermine legitimate government from within. Confronting instances of illegal trade therefore would mean confronting influential government members of the KP itself who benefited from such illicit activities. In the case of Zimbabwe, it also implied a challenge to the political security of those interests enabling and benefiting from the trade.

Hard, enduring and costly: diamonds and political transitions

Nearing the end of the GPA in 2013, after nearly 7 years of intense factional competition and gradual consolidation of control over mining and export operations, Marange diamonds presented a sobering illustration of the emergence of politically linked elite business and security networks of accumulation in Zimbabwe. The illegal diamond trade became inextricably bound up with Zimbabwe's troubled transition to a democratic, inclusive and stable political dispensation; failure to introduce transparency and accountability to the diamond sector implied a parallel defeat of democratic forces within the GPA government. The political and economic autonomy afforded some sections of the security forces and ZANU-PF by their privileged access to Marange diamonds nurtured the foundations of a parallel, shadow axis of power within the fragile GNU. Included within that politically led alliance were a range of interests with complementary power assets, such as state security forces and factions of the ZANU-PF elite. Also included in the alliance were party-linked business entrepreneurs, bureaucrats and officials in state-based mining agencies, diamond traders and dealers based in black markets, regional businesses (including some with links to political and security interests in their home countries), informal and artisanal miners and traders, and some sectors of local communities in the diamond-bearing areas. The combined capacities of this coalition were anchored in the brutal disciplining and monitoring power of the security agencies, and the political, administrative and legal authority of the ministry. But they also included political support from powerful regional business and political allies.

The illegal trade especially strengthened militarised interests that fell under, but were not entirely accountable to, the new political dispensation. Diamonds injected new elements of violence into a fragile political dispensation by sustaining partisan capacities for violence. Indeed, Marange's partisan exploitation *required* the continued disruption of democratic administration, transparency and rule of law. According to some reports, which documented the labyrinth of overlapping holding companies with securocrat and ZANU-PF connections, Marange's off-budget revenues effectively financed a parallel government enabled by the strategic protection of ZANU-PF controlled sections of the GNU, whose two primary objectives were the safe guarding of access points to secretive elite accumulation and state power (Global Witness 2012).

Consequently, a core contradiction remained unresolved throughout the life of the GPA and was episodically highlighted in fights involving control over Marange. It was not in the strategic interests of ZANU-PF and its business–security allies to implement a power-sharing agreement that might enable a transition leading to free, fair and decisive elections, which ZANU-PF would very likely lose. A dysfunctional GPA was required for secretive accumulation – and the electoral politics of violence and intimidation that depended on it – to succeed. At the same time, strategic access to the 'legitimate' state, notably its security, mining and information agencies, was needed to defend and expand ZANU-PF political-economic claims and displace opposing interests. Analysts who called for sustained support for the disappointing GPA due to the absence of alternatives failed to understand that unwavering MDC participation served to undermine that party's own legitimacy, the health of productive sectors subjected to looting and attack by ZANU-PF partisans, and the consolidation of stability and peace in the run up to new national elections (Solidarity Peace Trust 2010; Pigou 2010). It should be no surprise, then, that some critics argued this one-sided entrenchment of militarised politics under the auspices of inclusive government was a model to be critiqued, not celebrated, and rescuing the democratic transition project required more pressure on, and confrontation with, partisan militarised interests, not their appeasement through concessions like dropping sanctions on rights abusers and perpetrators of political violence (Research and Advocacy Unit 2010).

In this context, the problem of the politically infused illicit diamond trade required a broader political solution; the restructuring and rebuilding of the GPA state itself, including the reform and re-professionalisation of state agencies, and institutionalisation of open and accountable systems of administration and management. This was not simply a matter of redressing the excesses of established ZANU-PF patronage, as some MDC officials, including Morgan Tsvangirai, appeared to suggest in their continuing frustration at the slowness of change under the GNU (Tsvangirai 2010). Rather the political economy of black markets and security–business networks embedded in sections of the state needed to be subjected to public scrutiny in order to expose and challenge their toxic consequences for power-sharing and democratically accountable government. Indeed, Marange diamonds demonstrated the risks of *not* addressing the roots of the patronage problem. While black market production flourished under the watch of security forces and ministry structures, the GNU failed to confront the matter of who was profiting from the diamonds, their linkages to and engagement with the broader political terrain, and the consequences for the security and stability of local communities in Marange and the national political economy.

GNU inaction and the seeming marginalisation of the MDC from the political centre of gravity of diamond policy raised new questions about the coherence of the new government, and also about the democratic content and legitimacy of the GPA overall. For example, despite reports in late 2009 indicating criminal smuggling syndicates operating in collusion with the ZNA continued unabated, and that coerced labour, violent assault and torture, extralegal detentions and forced relocation of Chiadzwa communities persisted in the diamond fields, the Joint Monitoring and Implementation Committee – the structure set up under the GPA to monitor its implementation and address issues of human security and rights abuses – was effectively silent on the Marange chaos, and wholly irrelevant in addressing the complaints of civil society and rights organisations. Meanwhile, the MDC-controlled Ministry of Finance complained openly and fruitlessly about its inability to obtain basic data on diamond production revenues from the ZANU-PF controlled Ministry of Mines, and about the negative impacts of diamond revenue shortfalls on efforts to finance upcoming elections in the short term, and a reconstruction and development programme in the longer term.

By 2013, it was revealed by the finance ministry and subsequently confirmed by the ZANU-PF led Parliamentary Portfolio Committee on Minerals and Energy that only a fraction of earnings by diamond miners were actually deposited in the national treasury: for example, of the US $117m Mbada claimed to have paid to government in dividends in 2012, only US $41m was recorded by the Ministry of Finance as having been deposited. Moreover, additional fees, duties and taxes reported by Mbada were not registered as having arrived at the treasury at all (MDC 2013; Parliament of Zimbabwe 2013). Just as shocking was the Committee's revelation that it had been banned from visiting the Marange fields for more than 2 years during its investigation of Marange, and that official requests for information and testimony from the Ministry and public institutions under its control, and all diamond mining houses apart from Mbada, had been met with concerted obstruction: including silence, harassment, non-cooperation and occasionally, criminal misrepresentation in the content of the information provided. The pall of secrecy, corruption and suspicion surrounding Marange only thickened when Edward Chindori-Chinginga, ZANU-PF MP and Chairman of the Portfolio Committee, was killed in a mysterious car crash 1 week after tabling his Committee's damning report in Parliament and amid well-sourced evidence that he would not be permitted by his party to stand as a candidate in the upcoming 2013 elections (Gonda 2013; Bell 2013).

Conclusion

After a decade of intense partisan incursions by ZANU-PF linked political, security and business elites, the prospects for the wider non-partisan regularisation and supervision of the productive sector seemed increasingly remote as the GNU drew to a close in mid-2013. Against this backdrop, the political economy of Marange diamonds can be seen as a microcosm of the challenges posed by overlapping political, economic and security networks cemented by ZANU-PF in the 2000s. If results of the GPA's Marange 'litmus test' were sobering for the prospects of a democratic transition in Zimbabwe, they also pointed to new and complex webs of interests across Southern and East Africa which represent potential obstacles for movements calling for greater political participation and economic equity.

The lessons from Zimbabwe have been disheartening, and underline the residual survival and creative capacities of nationalist ruling elites and the sometimes-criminalised networks of accumulation which have emerged under their watch. A crucial remaining question is whether anyone or any institution, in southern Africa or beyond, has the political interest, commitment and means to challenge this situation. This article has shown that the regional proliferation of late-nationalist regimes, each with their own networks of politically brokered accumulation assembled behind veils of corruption and concealment, the fall out of market excesses and ineffective supervisory regulation, and the weak and halting interventions of internationally mandated bodies, suggest that the struggle to recoup popular control over Marange's diamond fields, and over democratic transitions more broadly, will be a long, deep and arduous one.

Note

1. The appointment of the MDC's Tendai Biti as the new Minister of Finance proved significant not only in the increased supervision of and transparent control over regular state finances including foreign donor flows but also in the marginalisation of RBZ Governor Gideon Gono, who had previously played a central role in sustaining ZANU-PF's partisan agenda through cloudy and ad hoc monetary and lending policies.

References

Bell, Alex. 2009. "Zim Diamond Ban 'Unlikely' as Government Argues Lack of Evidence." *SWRadioAfrica*. November 4. http://www.swradioafrica.com/news041109/zimdiamondban041109.htm.

Bell, Alex. 2013. "Chindori-Chininga Family Insist Fatal 'Accident' was Murder." *SWRadioAfrica*, June 27. http://allafrica.com/stories/201306280259.html.

Brief for Sub-National. 2010. JOC by Assistant Commissioner Mawere N. on Operation Hakudzokwi Phase VII. Leaked and published on numerous Zimbabwe-focused websites. May 7.

BusinessMap. 2001. *SADC Investor Survey 2001: Opportunities in Waiting*. Johannesburg.

Chikane, Abbey. 2010. "Second Fact Finding Mission Report." *Kimberley Process*, May 24–28.

Gagnon, Georgette. 2009. "Diamond Monitoring Body's Failure to Suspend Allows for Sale of 'Blood Diamonds'." *Human Rights Watch Press Statement*, November 6. www.hrw.org.

Global Witness. 2010. "Return of the Blood Diamond: The Deadly Race to Control Zimbabwe's New-found Diamond Wealth." June 14. http://www.globalwitness.org/library/return-blood-diamond-deadly-race-control-zimbabwes-new-found-diamond-wealth.

Global Witness. 2011. "Why we are Leaving the Kimberley Process – A Message from Global Witness Founding Director Charmian Gooch." December 5. http://www.globalwitness.org/library/why-we-are-leaving-kimberley-process-message-global-witness-founding-director-charmian-gooch.

Global Witness. 2012. "Financing a Parallel Government? The Involvement of the Secret Police and Military in Zimbabwe's Diamond, Cotton and Property Sectors." June. http://inec.usip.org/resource/financing-parallel-government-involvement-secret-police-and-military-zimbabwe%E2%80%99s-diamond-cot.

Gonda, Violet. 2013. "ZANU-PF Diamond Whistleblower Chindori-Chininga Dies in Car Crash." *SWRadioAfrica*, June 21. http://www.swradioafrica.com/2013/06/20/zanu-pfs-diamond-whistleblower-chindori-chininga-dies-in-car-crash.

Hammar, Amanda, and Brian Raftopoulos. 2003. *Zimbabwe's Unfinished Business: Rethinking Land, State and Nation in the Context of Crisis*. Harare: Weaver Press.

Hawkins, Tony. 2009. *The Mining Sector in Zimbabwe and its Potential Contribution to Recovery*. Harare: United Nations Development Program.

Human Rights Watch. 2008. "'Bullets for Each of You': State-sponsored Violence since Zimbabwe's March 29 Elections." June. http://www.hrw.org/reports/2008/06/09/bullets-each-you.

Human Rights Watch. 2009. "Diamonds in the Rough: Human Rights Abuses in the Marange Diamond Fields of Zimbabwe." June. http://www.hrw.org/reports/2009/06/26/diamonds-rough.

Kimberley Process. n.d. "Background." Accessed August 31. http://www.kimberleyprocess.com/background/index_en.html.

Kimberley Process. 2007. "Report of the Review Visit of the Kimberley Process to the Republic of Zimbabwe." May 29–June 1, 2007.

Kimberley Process. 2009. "Kimberley Process Certification Scheme Review Mission to Zimbabwe." June 30–July 4, 2009, Final Report.

MDC [Movement for Democratic Change]. 2013. "Minister Biti Concerned over Missing Diamond Revenue." May 28. http://allafrica.com/stories/201305290190.html.

Moyo, Andrew. 2009. "CIO Wants Me Silenced at KP Summit." *ZimOnline*, November 5. www.zimonline.co.za.

Mukumbira, Rodrick. 2006. "AIM Listed Zimbabwe Diamond Miner Evicted from its Claims." *Mineweb*. December 12. http://mineweb.com/mineweb/content/en/mineweb-historical-daily-news?oid=16611&sn=Detail.

Nyaira, Sandra. 2009a. "Zimbabwe Delegation to Kimberley Meeting in Namibia Said to Threaten NGOs." *Voice of America*, November 3. http://www.voanews.com.

Nyaira, Sandra. 2009b. "Kimberley Process Chair Defends Recent Decision Not to Suspend Zimbabwe." *Voice of America*, November 20. http://www.voanews.com.

Nyaira, Sandra. 2010. "Zimbabwe Activists Pressure Harare for Accountability on Diamond Operations." *Voice of America*, May 14. http://www1.voanews.com.

Nyamunda, Tinash, and Patience Mukwambo. 2012. "The State and the Bloody Diamond Rush in Chiadzwa." *Journal of Southern African Studies* 38 (1): 145–166. doi:10.1080/03057070.2012.649945.

Parliament of Zimbabwe. 2013. "Portfolio Committee on Mines and Energy." *First Report on Diamond Mining (with Special Reference to Marange Diamond Fields) 2009–2013*, presented to Parliament June 2013.

Partnership Africa Canada. 2009a. *Zimbabwe, Diamonds and the Wrong Side of History*. Ottawa: Partnership Africa Canada. http://www.pacweb.org/Documents/diamonds_KP/18_Zimbabwe-Diamonds_March09-Eng.pdf.

Partnership Africa Canada. 2009b. *Diamonds and Human Security: Annual Review 2009*. Ottawa: Partnership Africa Canada. http://www.pacweb.org/Documents/annual-reviews-diamonds/AR_diamonds_2009_eng.pdf.

Partnership Africa Canada. 2010. *Diamonds and Clubs: The Militarized Control of Diamonds and Power in Zimbabwe*. Ottawa: Partnership Africa Canada. http://www.pacweb.org/Documents/diamonds_KP/Zimbabwe-Diamonds_and_clubs-eng-June2010.pdf.

Partnership Africa Canada. 2012. *Reap What You Sow: Greed and Corruption in Zimbabwe's Marange Diamond Fields*. Ottawa. http://www.pacweb.org/en/pac-media/press-releases/184-new-pac-report-reap-what-you-sow-greed-and-corruption-in-zimbabwe-s-marange-diamond-fields.

Pigou, Piers. 2010. "Zimbabwe's Transition: Fact or Fantasy?" *The Thinker* 17: 36–39.

Raftopoulos, Brian. 2009. "The Crisis in Zimbabwe 1998-2008." In *Becoming Zimbabwe: A History from the Pre-colonial Period to 2008*, edited by Brian Raftopoulos and Alois Mlambo, 201–232. Harare: Weaver Press.

Research and Advocacy Unit. 2010. *What Are the Options for Zimbabwe? Dealing with the Obvious!* Harare, May 4. http://archive.kubatana.net/html/archive/demgg/100504rau.asp?sector=.

Sachikonye, Lloyd. 2007. "Diamonds in Zimbabwe: A Situational Analysis." *Resource Insight Issue*, May 1. http://archive.revenuewatch.org/reports/DIamondZimb.pdf.

Saul, John S., and Richard Saunders. 2005. "Mugabe, Gramsci and Zimbabwe at 25." *International Journal* (Toronto) 60: 953–975. doi:10.2307/40204093.

Saunders, Richard. 2007. *Mining and Crisis in Zimbabwe*. Amsterdam: Niza/Fatal Transactions.

Saunders, Richard. 2008. "Crisis, Capital, Compromise: Mining and Empowerment in Zimbabwe." *African Sociological Review* 12 (1): 67–89.

Saunders, Richard. 2009. *Briefing Note: Conflict Diamonds from Zimbabwe*. Amsterdam: Niza/Fatal Transactions. http://www.bicc.de/fataltransactions/pdf/briefing_note_conflict_diamonds_from_zimbabwe.pdf.

Saunders, Richard. 2010. "The Modern Face of Conflict Diamonds: Lessons from Zimbabwe." Paper presented at Pathfinder 2010 Conference, 'Illegal Trade in Natural Resources: What Can Brussels Do?' Brussels, September 30.

Sixholo, Ndodana. 2010. "Israeli Funding Zim Diamond Mining." *ZimOnline*, April 20. www.zimonline.co.za.

Smillie, Ian. 2010. "Ian Smillie Addresses Human Rights, Diamonds and the Kimberley Process." *Rapaport News*, September 10. www.diamonds.net/news/NewsItem.aspx?ArticleID=27951.

Solidarity Peace Trust. 2010. "What Options for Zimbabwe?" *Johannesburg*, March 31. http://www.solidaritypeacetrust.org/download/report-files/what_options_for_Zimbabwe.pdf.

Tsvangirai, Morgan. 2010. *PM this Week*, Edition 45, June 2.

Vircoulon, Thierry. 2010. "Time to Rethink the Kimberley Process: The Zimbabwe Case." *International Crisis Group*, November 4. www.crisisgroup.org.

Zimbabwe Chamber of Mines. 2009. *Annual Report 2008*. Harare, May. http://www.chamber-ofminesofzimbabwe.com/publications.html.

Zimbabwe Lawyers for Human Rights, Centre for Research and Development, Zimbabwe Environmental Lawyers Association, Counselling Services Unit and Zimbabwe Association of Doctors for Human Rights. 2009. Untitled submission to KP Review Mission, June.

Ziyera, Enddy. 2007. "A Handful of Dust: The Diamond Saga in Zimbabwe." *Break Free: Monthly Newsletter of Zimbabwe Coalition on Debt and Development*, March. www.sarpn.org.za.

Index

Note: Page numbers followed by 'n' refer to notes